T0062969

You Can Soar with Angels

A Humorous Approach to a Serious Subject

A. XAVIER SUSTAETA

BALBOA
PRESS

A DIVISION OF HAY HOUSE

Copyright © 2014 Angel Xavier Sustaeta.

All rights reserved. No part of this book may be used or reproduced by any means, graphic, electronic, or mechanical, including photocopying, recording, taping or by any information storage retrieval system without the written permission of the publisher except in the case of brief quotations embodied in critical articles and reviews.

Balboa Press books may be ordered through booksellers or by contacting:

Balboa Press
A Division of Hay House
1663 Liberty Drive
Bloomington, IN 47403
www.balboapress.com
1 (877) 407-4847

Because of the dynamic nature of the Internet, any web addresses or links contained in this book may have changed since publication and may no longer be valid. The views expressed in this work are solely those of the author and do not necessarily reflect the views of the publisher, and the publisher hereby disclaims any responsibility for them.

The author of this book does not dispense medical advice or prescribe the use of any technique as a form of treatment for physical, emotional, or medical problems without the advice of a physician, either directly or indirectly. The intent of the author is only to offer information of a general nature to help you in your quest for emotional and spiritual well-being. In the event you use any of the information in this book for yourself, which is your constitutional right, the author and the publisher assume no responsibility for your actions.

Any people depicted in stock imagery provided by Thinkstock are models, and such images are being used for illustrative purposes only. Certain stock imagery © Thinkstock.

Printed in the United States of America.

ISBN: 978-1-4525-2404-7 (sc)
ISBN: 978-1-4525-2405-4 (e)

Balboa Press rev. date: 11/19/2014

CONTENTS

*"It has become apparently obvious that our technology
has exceeded our humanity"* - Albert Einstein

*"And now, here is my secret, a very simple secret: it is only
with the heart that one can see rightly, what is essential
is invisible to the eye"*- Antoine de Saint-Exupery

"Believe you can, and you are halfway there" - Theodore Roosevelt

"Comedy is simply a funny way of being serious" - Peter Ustinov

"I am trying to shut up and let my Angels speak to me and tell me what I am supposed to do" - Patrick Swayze

"Faith is a knowledge within the heart beyond the reach of proof" - Khalil Gibran

"As my mind can conceive of more good, the barriers and blocks dissolve. My life becomes full of little miracles popping out of the blue" – Louis L. Hay

"There is always room for a story that can transport people to another place" - J.K. Rowling

"We are, each of us, Angels with only one wing, and we can only fly by embracing one another" - Luciano de Crescenzo

"You have to work hard to get your thinking clean, to make it simple. But it's worth it in the end because once you get there, you can move mountains" - Steve Jobs

"You have to take risks. We will only understand the miracle of life fully when we allow the unexpected to happen" – Paolo Coelho

"Try to be the rainbow in someone's cloud" – Maya Angelou

PREFACE

"Humor is something that thrives between man's aspirations and his limitations. There is more logic in humor than in anything else because, you see, humor is truth" - Victor Borge

Over the centuries Angels have become demystified - which is good, but most of this has been at the expense of their severe devaluation - which is not so good. Their status has declined from messengers of God to folklore characters, one notch below Santa Claus - Angels not having a fixed gift-delivery appointment in our calendars.

Furthermore, competition is tough for air space nowadays. Commercial and civil flights are crowding the skies. TSA is imposing more and more air travel restrictions. No-Fly zones are more prevalent each day. Even Clark Kent is having a tough time keeping his audience, now heavily skewed towards the newly redrawn Marvel superheroes in their 3D, pixel-enhanced screen appearances. To cope with, and survive all of this, Angels have had to evolve, and we must now learn to recognize them in their present form.

Hopefully, this book can restore some Angel credibility by providing a fresh and lighthearted approach to their wonderfully simple ways, and their interaction with us in our daily lives. It was conceived as a down-to-earth, personal-experience-based testimonial of basic, often forgotten.... but always evergreen truths regarding our own spirituality, and by logical extension, that of Angels, and our relationship to them.

Having enjoyed several encounters with Angels (none of them winged), all resulting in profound life changes, the author felt compelled to give testimony of his experiences in an effort to invite other people to rekindle their belief, and perhaps to even consider picking up some Angel qualities along the way.

The author makes frequent use of quotes from notable and varied sources. This is not only to support and enlighten the sections where they are included, but more importantly, they serve as sources of reflection on the topics at hand, whilst often adding some humor.

There are 12 chapters in this book, each independent of the others, but integrally linked in the structure of the book, forming a compendium - in the same manner that we are each individual beings, but are connected to each other as part of the whole of humanity…..the planet…..and ultimately, the universe.

The initial chapters provide some socioeconomic reflections as to how and why Angels have fallen "out of grace" with us. The subsequent chapters offer insights as to how we may restore their good office in our lives, and are interlaced with three Angel short stories.

It is the author's intent to present some fundamental truths in such a way that the earnest, open-minded and open-hearted reader will rediscover them as already present in their hearts, and thus empower himself/herself to shed all fears and guilt; to refocus on correct priorities; and to open the path for reclaiming internal peace and contentment. In short, to live life as it was meant to be: as divine manifestations of the supreme - as integral parts of a whole.

By validating these truths, or better said: by **re-validating** these truths, and by being willing and committed to live by them - discarding all the false knowledge and values imbued through generations of misguided social, and political patterns, we can once again **re-imagine** ourselves in our **true image**. And then, but only then.....can we gracefully soar with the Angels - for we can also be one.

As it is above, so is below.

To quote Lao Tzu: *"At the center of your being you have the answer; you know who you are, and you know what you want".....*

and Andre Gide: *"Be faithful to that which exists within yourself"*

CLARIFICATION:

This book IS NOT a religious dissertation. This book IS NOT a collection of angelic visitations. This book IS NOT an attempt to convert, persuade, or in any way seduce readers to increase their expectations of experiencing any form of apparitions – angelic, or other, as they are portrayed in the Old....and New Testaments. Allegorical burning bushes and chariots of fire ARE NOT part of the author's field of interest.

"Imagination was given to man to compensate him for what he is not, and a sense of humor to console him for what he is" - Francis Bacon

CHAPTER I

The Reason Angels Went the Way of Blockbuster

"It has become apparently obvious that our technology has exceeded our humanity" - Albert Einstein

If you are under 30 years of age, the world is your oyster. You are fully in tune with, and dependent upon all the modern tools that have become ritualistic in your day-to-day lives. By "tools", I am referring to smart phones, tablets, apps, twitter, Facebook, Instagram, e-books, Netflix, iTunes, uploading, downloading, Googling, pirating, cloning, etc... etc... You know....the well-known "tools" that are needed for daily life, and in whose absence you may perish socially.

If you are over 30 years of age, but less than 50, you must have already sensed that it feels like time is going by faster and faster each year, but this is a challenge that you find exhilarating, and necessary in order to be "on the edge". Life is wonderful....you never had more fun things to do without having to go anywhere, and without having to do anything but look at the smart phone on the palm of your hand.

Conversely, if you are over 50, but under 65, you are well aware of these phenomena, and although you are enjoying a sense of wonderment at the rapid progress, you have perhaps also begun to develop some degree of concern about it. After all, how far, and to where are these changes leading us; and……more critical, for how long will you be able to keep up with them?

Lastly, if you are over 65 – which by the way, is no longer "old age" - at least not as far as actuarial statistics and quality of life indicate, you cannot help but feel, with some inadequacy, the vertiginous pace at which events are taking place; the constant introduction of new technologies; the ease with which new concepts and ideas are replacing their previous counterparts; and the necessity of accepting the omnipresent reality of short-term, built-in obsolescence as endemic to all new goods. Thus, enforcing their constant replacement, and the ensuing proliferation of rampant consumerism as an established way of life. A cynic would correctly point out that Buddha was right when teaching that nothing is permanent

The single most time-accelerating factor is communications: hardware / software / delivery / availability / reliability / scope. News events are shared world-wide on instant live-coverage basis - very often without censure of any kind; very often originating from unknown and unverified sources.

What is presently happening in Kabul – or in almost any other place of the world, can be reported and seen in New York, Tokyo, Mexico City, London…and in any small town and rural community - practically everywhere, as it takes place. This is not only as it refers to news reported by established/recognized news organizations, and watched in TV / laptops / tablets / smartphones, and a few more devices I may have left out. It can also be, as previously mentioned, privately and individually broadcast to the world via all kinds of social media, revealing images, along with uncensored personal narratives….and received by all of us in a nanosecond in one of our many devices. How do we separate fact from fiction?

Likewise, music can also be instantly downloaded or streamed by any of our many gadgets at any time we choose. Remember cassette tapes….. eight track systems ….turn tables…33's…45's…78's…?? All things of the past…yes, of the past 40 years!!! Some of us may also remember the days of having only one radio, or one record player in our entire household….or how about rotary dial phones? Now cell phones are all of the above, and better! And, everyone …everyone…. has a cell phone. Everybody is "in the loop". Modern society simply does not function without our electronic devices….our economy is based on them to the highest degree.

Putting things under some degree of perspective, and providing a clue as to the direction this narrative is taking, I will get closer to the point and explain: Progress forces societies and products to either evolve or perish. Likewise, Angels were confronted with the same paradigm centuries ago…..and they did evolve, hence survived - but to see them we cannot look for them in their original forms. We have to update our expectations, in the same manner that if we want to watch a particular movie at home, we should not expect to rent it in DVD format any longer; we now turn to Movies on Demand, or Netflix, or similar.

As the economies of the modern world progressed from farming to trading - to manufacturing - to assembling - to outsourcing - to distributing - to designing - to service - to consuming - to healthcare - to hospitality, to….etc…etc…, the entertainment industry proliferated and became one of the largest and most profitable conglomerates of our age, with movies, videos and music, being its core.

All of these rapid changes have had a profound effect on the very fabric of our society and our personal lives, not only as to what products and services we use and how we use them, but also, and perhaps more important, as to how we apply our time, and how we establish our priorities.

As it took several decades of film making for the entertainment industry to go from silent films to "talkies" – to Technicolor – to special effects – to multi-screen theaters….. and finally, to home entertainment, which is where we now spend most, if not all of our leisure time, it also took several decades for the communications industry to go from telegraph to telephone – to radio – to TV – to satellite – to fiber optics – to microwaves – to (?) whatever is the new "it".

However, fueled by new and rapidly changing technologies, these industries are now evolving so fast that they are transforming our lives continuously. Example: in the current decade, we have seen the birth, and demise, of the game-changer but short-lived Blackberry - the once indispensable tool for every businessman and hip socialite. However, although the brand had a short life span, the product concept itself – smart phone, evolved and survived. The brand (Blackberry) was soon replaced by other brands with new, better technologies: iPhones and Androids, which do more tasks and perform them better than the precursor product. With any of these brands we can literally have access to the world from the palm of our hand.

We have also seen the birth and evolution of laptops of great efficiency, and their transition into tablets, and smarter "smart phones" - both becoming indispensable tools in our work; in our studies; and in our leisure.

Concurrently, we have witnessed the downfall of the photo film industry (remember having a Kodak moment?) due to the explosive growth of digital cameras…now embodied in our cell phones and tablets.

One inevitable consequence of this progress is that the new technologies have made it almost impossible to differentiate - using the traditional definition of each, the communications industry from the entertainment industry, and from the news industry. In fact, all three industries, fueled by these technologies, have synergistically amalgamated, constituting such a powerful and controlling socioeconomic, behavior-changing force as has never been seen before.

The entertainment industry not only embraced, but practically absorbed the news industry. Yes, we can affirm that the news industry (the press) is now an integral component of the entertainment industry! Accordingly, trivial and often sordid information about a rock star or movie star; or for that matter, antics of a Honeyboobooesque or Octamomaesque character, are broadcast.....and viewed, as subjects of interest in our society.

Details of a common (but obscenely famous and rich) courtesan's marriage(s) generate millions of dollars via PR manipulations, taking precedent over news reports of global tragedies, and human indignities such as the institutionalized genocide in Syria, or the prevalent infanticide in India.

And when "real" news are reported, which is also constantly....and repeatedly, they are selected, formatted, and manipulated (sometimes even fabricated) in such a way as to increase media ratings, often at the expense of veracity and relevant content; always for the sake of viewer impact, and the resulting influence on public opinion. Remember WMD?

This may still sound like a digression from our topic, but it is not; actually it is its very root, for it exemplifies and defines the direction that our intellectual and moral compass is taking. When an alarmingly large portion of our society so avidly consumes these sensational and trivial "news" (here I am not talking of WMD – which falls into an altogether different moral category) at the expense of intellectual endeavors, and practically of all spiritual development, it is time to step back and review our priorities.

But, briefly getting back to the evolution of the film, music, and television industries: they synergistically transformed the entertainment industry, becoming conglomerates; creating and fueling a new business venue, one that provides bespoke entertainment to the home. In other words, a venture that allows us to view the films of our choice, at the time of our choice, at the location of our choice to the apparent detriment of movie theaters, but to the satisfaction of our insatiable appetite for entertainment, and clearly, to the great benefit of these conglomerates.

In the genesis of the home entertainment industry, Blockbuster was one of the pioneers, performing a wonderful and innovative service…. which, although eventually victimized by new technologies, thrived for a decade or so until the lighting-speed momentum of progress brought us to the digital age where new and better entertainment formats, with new delivery systems were born: Netflix – initially in discs sent by post – a now anachronistic concept, and then in downloads/streaming…. and YouTube…. and Movies On Demand, etc…etc….In short, Blockbuster died as a brand, but the concept – home entertainment, evolved and thrives thanks to the same technologies that made Blockbuster obsolete. I employ Blockbuster as a prominent example of many such fatalities only for its undisputed, memorable, and transformative value, but the brand cemetery is full of similar corpses.

For the sake of nostalgia, can we remember a single strip center where there was not a Blockbuster (or similar) outlet 15 years ago…..in any state…in any town…. in almost any "civilized" country? Of course not, they were everywhere. They were to home movies what Starbucks is to coffee: synonyms of social lubricants - with one difference being that the former was exclusively for takeout, and the latter is greatly for in-premise consumption - with its niche being as much the product it sells, as the atmosphere it offers for its consumption. Perhaps one could even venture to ponder if Starbucks is a niche of the entertainment industry, since it offers a place to see and be seen…a place to avail oneself of communications technology (Wi-Fi), and therefore use our "tools" to communicate and entertain ourselves.

So when I say that the Angels "went the way of Blockbuster", I simply mean that they were both victims of "progress", and the resulting changes that come about, particularly as these changes relate to our use of time.

With paradoxical similitudes, but at a much slower pace - a period of time spanning centuries and not decades, Angels, in their biblical and historical formats/castings, gradually faded as societies became better defined, more complex, and evolved - particularly in their use of non-working time. Gazing at the firmament on a starry night, pondering the wonders of creation, became less and less frequent as cities populated and our activities changed from pastoral to commercial, to industrial, to technological.

However, the divine essence of Angels, like the concept of home entertainment, also evolved and survived. But unlike the Blockbuster brand name that was quickly replaced, Angels, enjoying a technology-free habitat, continued to exist under the same brand name - albeit a new logo design and up-to-date packaging, making them highly present if the audience is willing to look in the right places - which do not include TV screens.

Modern times do not require us to be prophets or members of the "chosen tribe" to experience encounters with Angels. And when such encounters take place, the Angel is most likely not going to be a luminous winged creature surrounded by trumpet bearing cherubim. It is either going to come in the subtle form an inner voice, a dream, or a helping hand...often from a stranger - always at the precise time of need; leaving us with no doubt, especially in our heart, that it was an Angel indeed.

All we have to do is to go back to basics: We must pay a little more attention to our hearts; a little less to our intellectual minds, and a lot less to our "tools".

Angels are all around us….and we can enjoy them if we could only be still for a moment and open ourselves to their presence…..allow for their presence.

Here are some interesting reflections from worthier sources:

"We are born, we live for a brief instant, and we die. It's been happening for a long time. Technology is not changing it much – if at all" - Steve Jobs

"Technological society has succeeded in multiplying the opportunities for pleasure, but it has great difficulty generating joy" - Pope Paul IV

"We have more media than ever and more technology in our lives. It's supposed to help us communicate, but it has the opposite effect of isolating us" - Tracy Chapman

"I think technology really increased human ability. But technology cannot produce compassion" - Dalai Lama

"If we continue to develop our technology without wisdom or prudence, our servant may prove to be our executioner" - Omar N. Bradley

"The internet is so big, so powerful, that for some people it is a complete substitute for life". - Andrew Brown

"I force people to have coffee with me, just because I don't trust that a friendship can be maintained without any other senses besides a computer or cell phone screen" - John Cusack

"You affect the world by what you watch" - Tim Berners-Lee

CHAPTER II

We Must Put Our Hearts to Full Use

"And now, here is my secret, a very simple secret: it is only
with the heart that one can see rightly, what is essential
is invisible to the eye"- Antoine de Saint-Exupery

What is a heart? Really…..please let's think about this for a moment. We know that it is a vital organ….arguably, the most vital organ in our body. But is that all it is?

From the physiological point of view, as vital as the heart is to our body, its anatomical / text book description is not much different from that of any other organ in our body, as it is exclusively concerned with (a) consistency and tissue components; (b) function (pumping blood); and (c) location within our body. In other words, to the medical student - or for that matter, to anyone interested in learning about the anatomy of the heart, the heart is nothing but an organ that provides one of the two most necessary life-sustaining functions for all species with a circulatory system.

However, in spite of this well understood specific physiological function, the heart has been universally portrayed and recognized for centuries as the epicenter of our strongest emotions, love in particular. When we fall in love, we fall in love with our heart; and when something goes emotionally amiss, we have it "broken". Why is it that out greatest joys, as well as our greatest sorrows are experienced in/by the heart…..what makes it so uniquely different from other organs, that it indisputably monopolizes our romantic emotions? Why instead, do we not say to the object of our affection that "we love them with our pancreas"; or why not say when ditched by that loved one, that he/she "broke our liver"?

Well…..it just does not *"feel"* right to say it, does it? It makes no sense. Thus, there has to be more to the heart than what meets the eye when reading its anatomical / physiological description, which is something like this:

> *"The heart is a hollow muscular organ that pumps blood throughout the blood vessels to various parts of the body by repeated, rhythmic contractions. It is found in all animals with a circulatory system, which includes the vertebrates. The average human heart, beating at 72 beats per minute, will beat approximately 3.5 billion times during an average 85 year lifespan, and pumps approximately 4.7 – 5.7 liters of blood per minute. The adult human heart has a mass of between 250 and 350 grams and is about the size of a fist. It is located anterior to the vertebral column and posterior to the sternum. It is enclosed in a double-walled sac called the pericardium. This outer wall is composed of three layers; the outer layer is called the epicardium; the middle layer is called the myocardium, and is composed of contractile cardiac muscle; and the inner layer is called the endocardium……"*

Is there any justification stemming from this anatomical description / definition of the human heart that can even remotely link it to our feelings of love…or sorrow?

Let's compare it to the anatomical / biological description of a pancreas, and see if perhaps we find a clue there:

> *"The pancreas is a glandular organ in the digestive system and endocrine system of vertebrates. In humans it is located in the abdominal cavity behind the stomach. It is an endocrine gland producing several important hormones, including insulin, glucagon, somatostatin and pancreatic polypeptides which circulate in the blood. The pancreas is also a digestive organ, secreting pancreatic juice containing digestive enzymes that assist digestion and absorption of nutrients in the small intestines. These enzymes help to further break down the carbohydrates, proteins and lipids....."*

Based on these definitions, could one of the two organs, heart or pancreas, be more logically linked to romance than the other? I fail to see any connection, but if pressed, I would be inclined to nominate the pancreas as love's fulcrum, as it deals with insulin, hence glucose, i.e sugar....and love is indeed sweet.

But clearly, it just does not *feel* right to tell our loved one that we love them with all our pancreas. The key word is **"*feel*"**. We simply do not "*feel*" with our pancreas...we do not "*feel*" with even our brain! We "*feel*" with our heart, and we "*feel*" with our gut, the other sensory receptor that governs our emotions and intuition. These two organs, in addition to their bodily functions, are simultaneously and respectively the source, and reservoir of our love, courage, common sense, and intuition. It is with our hearts, and only with our hearts, that we can recognize and enjoy the presence of Angels.

I know I can safely say, in spite of text book definitions of heart and gut, that we all intuitively agree there is more to these two anatomical components than what can be physiologically explained. Deepak Chopra has given us a very clear and succinct explanation:

> *"There are receptors to these molecules in your immune system, in your gut and in your heart. So when you say 'I have a gut feeling' or 'my heart is sad' or 'I am bursting with joy,' you are not speaking metaphorically. You are speaking literally".*

Contemporaneously, a fascinating scientific project, which some of you may be familiar with, is being done by the Institute of HeartMath Research Center (IHM) www.heartmath.org founded by Doc Childre in 1991 in Boulder Creek, California. As stated in their mission, their aim is to facilitate more balance and health in people by:

- Researching the effects of positive emotions on physiology quality of life, and performance
- Helping individuals engage their hearts to transform stress and rejuvenate their health
- Providing prevention and intervention strategies for improved emotional health, decision-making, learning skills and violence reduction in communities, families and schools

IHM is investigating the physiological means by which the heart actually communicates with the brain. How the heart influences the information process, as well as perceptions, emotions and health. They are asking questions such as why people experience the feeling of love and other emotional states in the area of the heart....what effect do our emotions have on the autonomic nervous system, and the hormonal and immune systems? All fascinating questions, and all germane to our quest for why is that the heart falls in love, and not the pancreas.

These questions represent the onset of a specific discipline: Neurocardiology, and as we can see in IHM's overview of their research, as reported in their Publication No. 01-001, compiled by Rollin McCraty, Mike Atkinson, and Dana Tomasino. Some of their reported findings indicate the following:

> *"The answers to our original questions now provide a scientific basis to explain how and why the heart affects mental clarity, creativity, emotional balance, and personal effectiveness. **Our research and that of others indicate that the heart is far more than a simple pump.** The heart is in fact, a highly complex, self-organized information processing center with its own functional "brain" that communicates with and influences the cranial brain via the nervous system, hormonal system and other pathways.....As a critical nodal point in many of the body's interacting systems, **the heart is uniquely positioned as a powerful entry point in the communication network that connects body, mind, emotions, and spirit"**.*

Even more fascinating, are IHM's reports concerning the energetic communication of the heart, referred to as *cardioelectromagnetic communication.*

One of their findings:

> *"The heart is the most powerful generator of electromagnetic energy in the human body, producing the largest rhythmic electromagnetic field of any of the body's organs. The heart's electrical field is about 60 times greater in amplitude than the electrical activity generated by the brain..... furthermore, the magnetic field produced by the heart is more than 5,000 times greater in strength than the field generated by the brain, and can be detected a number of feet away from the body, in all directions".*

These are indeed exiting findings, and are opening new pathways to better understand our human physiology in a holistic spectrum. But still, can our "feelings" and "hunches" be fully understood, justified, and explained in a rational, intellectual, and pragmatic manner? No, not to most people. The intellect is not involved in this matter. But, does this make them less real?

I will quote Carl Sagan to respond: *"Absence of evidence is not evidence of absence"* to which I would add: How do YOU *"feel"* when you read these statements about intuition, and about our heart being the center of our emotions? Do they have resonance with you ....do they represent a truism in your belief system; in your core; in your experience?

Or do you find heart-felt and gut-felt intuition and emotions to be mere usurpers of a subconscious genius that produces and governs our thoughts and feelings, relegating other alternatives as fodder for dreamers? If you do the latter, I suggest that, if you have not already done so, you stop reading this book and not waste any further time on it, as it deals with intangibles, it deals with matters of the heart…matters of the gut…. matters of faith. And it deals with simple common sense; often – if not always, relying precisely on intuition and love.

To substantiate, to those readers still with me, how one of the most successful and recognized contemporary achievers bases his decisions on gut feelings, followed by subsequent in-depth analysis when it comes to business - I am sure, I will share some words from Sir Richard Branson, founder of the Virgin Group:

> *"I never get the accountants in before I start up a business.*
> *It's all done on gut feeling, especially if I can see that they*
> *are taking the mickey out of the consumer".*

Sir Richard is perhaps the most practical example of how we should follow our instincts, and our hearts. He has, following his heart and his gut (showing plenty of the latter), created one of the world's largest business empires, the Virgin Group, encompassing more than 400 companies in many industries, ranging from transportation (Virgin Air, Virgin Rail and now Virgin Galactic) to entertainment (Virgin Records) to banking, to retailing amongst many.

But he is not all business, he is, I dare say, all adventure and all dreams – most brought to fruition, as his other triumphs attest, by following his heart, and fueled by his guts. To list two of many: he holds a world record for crossing the Atlantic in a hot air balloon; and is an accomplished world class sailor, holding several transoceanic records. But, why do I say so much about this man? Because he exemplifies what one man can accomplish in a single lifetime by having the guts to follow his heart.

This last sentence encapsulates the intent of this book: to motivate you to follow your heart; to open it; to have the guts to attain the completion of your goal; and to empower you to recognize and honor you intuitions - for if you do these, you will certainly encounter Angels in your path.

As motivation for all of us, I am including a few pertinent quotes:

"Your time is limited....have the courage to follow your heart and intuition" - Steve Jobs

"There is no instinct like that of the heart" – Lord Byron

"Everyone has been made for some particular work, and the desire for that work has been put in every heart" - Rumi

"Only do what your heart tells you" - Princes Diana

"Wherever you go, go with all your heart" - Confucius

CHAPTER III

To Fly, We Must First Trim Our Ballast

"Believe you can, and you are halfway there" - Theodore Roosevelt

The heavier the load, the greater the effort needed to move it. This is an irrefutable axiom that holds true for any activity. One of the best examples of this can be observed in the automotive industry. In order to meet current Federal and State Emission Standards, automotive manufacturers have been forced to make significant improvements to the two main factors involved:

1. Weight reduction
2. Better propulsion systems, i.e. cleaner fuels, and more efficient combustion engines

The result of these changes is that today's automobiles, being much lighter and having more efficient engines, using cleaner fuels, can travel much faster and farther, whilst consuming significantly less fuel and emitting less pollutants than the old clunkers of a few years back.

The same principle applies to all us for any positive advancement to take effect, whether it be physical, intellectual, emotional, or spiritual advancement. If we do indeed want to move to higher planes; if we do indeed want to soar to greater heights, we must follow the automotive industry's example and not remain old clunkers weighted down by excess loads, especially in the form of shiny ostentatious cladding. Equally important, we must re-think the type of fuel we are giving our body, our brain, our hearts, and our souls.

First, let's get started in this quest by reducing the amount of "luggage" we carry. By this, I mean all the unnecessary memories and feelings that we carry on our minds and on our shoulders from past experiences… some of them being rooted in hurt; others in guilt; others in nostalgia; others in insecurity; and others that have been passed on to us from previous generations - most of them having no use to us other than burdening us and making our path more tortuous. We must discard the old in order to make room for the new.

If you are still hurting because you feel that your first employer was unfair when he overpassed you in promotions….LET IT GO. It does not really matter. It is not important. It has no bearing on your life any longer.

You are where you are. You are in today…. in this moment - not in yesterday; not in any other day. Focus only in today, and do not look back at what could have been. Always remember that the only people, and the only experiences that can hurt us, are those that we allow to do so.

Eject from your life all past hindrances…keep only the good things, but even regarding those, be careful not to dwell on them for too long. Allow good memories to sweeten your life, but do not become their slave by living in the past, for they will preclude you from acquiring new ones. Live and enjoy the present, for that is all you have…and that is all you need!

Secondly, let's also, like automobile industry did, change the quality of the fuels (nourishment) we are using, for both, our physical sustenance, as well as for our intellectual and spiritual growth. For the former, we must stop eating "junk" foods, and substitute them with healthy natural alternatives that can provide our bodies with healthier nutrients and be free of toxins.

The food industry has practically destroyed the wholeness and nutritional value of its goods by focusing on shelf life; cost effective distribution; persuasive packaging; and, above all, by being exclusively driven by profit margins – by greed.

Take a few minutes before buying your groceries and read the labels. You will find that some of the "ingredients" are unpronounceable to anyone other than chemists. Instead buy fresh products. Buy lots of leafy greens and bright colored vegetables. Nature put those colors there for a reason, the brighter and wider variety of colors you consume, the better balanced your diet will be.

Eat more fish and less meat. When buying poultry make sure it is hormone free. Do the same with milk and eggs. Buy as much organics as you can. I know they are more expensive, but we are talking about your health. Use real butter instead of margarine. Use only extra virgin olive oil. And last but certainly not least, dramatically cut down on sweets – completely eliminating artificial sweeteners.

It is critical that you become conscious of the simple fact that we are what we eat. If we eat junk food (this prominently includes all processed foods), our bodies become "junky". If we eat healthy foods, these will be metabolized into a healthy body.

But I do not want to dwell too much on our poor eating habits – the point has been made; or on the mendacity of the food industry, as this is a topic of another book, one in which I would vent against the criminal use of GMOs, the abuse of preservatives, pesticides, etc…etc…..all of them greed-based technologies that are killing us whilst lining their pockets. Other, much better qualified authors are already performing this educational process, and the results seem to be very promising, as each day more and more people take control over their food dollars and are spending them in better alternatives.

Our awakening to this reality is taking place....I urge you to join the movement.

Accordingly, let's go back to the subject at hand and focus on the "other" nourishment, or better said, lack of nourishment, that is afflicting our society: Intellectual and spiritual nourishment - both in dire absence from our average daily life. Sadly, many of us have completely eliminated the much needed sustenance that our intellects and our souls require for our evolvement and unfoldment.

We largely function in "auto pilot" throughout our days, performing our tasks in a mechanically efficient / semi-robotic fashion; in a state of intellectual and spiritual lethargy. We are so engrossed in our physical lives, that we have abandoned all higher pursuits, falling victims to our routines, without ever pausing to actually think about anything other than work, social life, comfort, and leisure - things superfluous to our divine essence. This surrender to our lazy habits is akin to a slow intellectual and spiritual suicide by starvation.

Let's ask ourselves: When was the last time you got up early for the purpose of watching the sunrise....or had the enjoyment to quietly savor a sunset...or take a walk in the woods with no companion other than yourself? Did you notice the smile on the face of that child skipping rope....or the sadness of the old lonely lady quietly shuffling towards her empty home? Are you aware of other people...and are you appreciative of the beauty, and the desolation that surrounds you?

So, in addition to changing our eating habits let's also change our "free time" habits. Let's put a stop to reading and watching the "garbage" that comes our way on a constant basis in the form of gossip magazines, and gossip TV shows that do nothing but feed our lower intellects and base instincts.

I am not advocating puritanism, or that we all become so intellectualized that we no longer have time for a good healthy laugh provoked by a good healthy sitcom, or even better, by a good conversation. Quite the contrary, a good laugh is an indispensable ingredient for a happy life, and we should laugh many times each day. What I am advocating is that we be more selective, more intelligent in our choices; that we not fall easy targets to the greed of publishers and producers that prey on man's tendency for the shallow, for the morbid, and for the spectacular.

The key word is MODERATION. Extremes are very bad. Eating 100% healthy, 100% of the time; never indulging in any small digression – like a good ice cream, although obviously better than not eating healthy, can be extremely boring (remember that we are what we eat!), and is not something that I would follow, as my nature is one of partaking in all "good stuff" ....but with prudence.

Likewise, when it comes to intellectual and spiritual cultivation, we have to maintain a healthy balance and be light-hearted enough to enjoy a good walk in the park without necessarily making it a ritualistic walking meditation event – although doing one of these once in a while may pleasantly surprise you with its soothing value.

Let's substitute, at least partially in the beginning, our junky habits by starting to read at least 30 minutes per day some worthwhile pages... either fiction or in educational - good literature of any kind; certainly not the scandalous tabloids, and vain gossip magazines that infest the cashier lines at supermarkets.

And let's switch channels in our TVs: from "The Krudatians", or from "Fowl Dynasty" to something that will enrich our lives, and put a healthy smile on our faces; whether this is in the form of a cultural mini-series, or travel documentaries, or a good sit-com, or family oriented movies, or……anything with a positive content; with an uplifting influence. Let's choose programs that will enrich our lives, and not sabotage reality and pollute our minds as the mentioned shows do.

Let's also pay attention to the type of music we choose. Is it relaxing and inspirational, or does it excite and overstimulate you in a less than noble direction? Does it provoke an adrenalin rush, or a happy, tranquil feeling? Let your heart decide these issues, and have the will to follow your intuition. Discoing once in a while is good fun, but waltzing on other days is fundamental to our happiness. Let's do a little of both.

And finally, let's eliminate the BIGGEST contributor to our spiritual, emotional, and intellectual disenfranchisement: VIOLENCE.

Let's begin this section by asking ourselves a few simple questions:

- How reasonable is it to expect our youth to become loving, peaceful, compassionate, law abiding adults, if they are, from an early age, continuously fed violence: via their toys, their games, their music, their movies, their social media?
- How reasonable is it to expect a gentle, peaceful society, when we legally have arsenals of rapid-fire weapons in our homes, and demand our "right" to have even more?
- How reasonable is it to expect our nation to be a nation at peace when we have been involved in six (6) major wars in the past 65 years (WW II; Korea; Viet Nam; Kuwait; Iraq; Afghanistan), and several "minor incursions" into other countries?
- How reasonable is it to consider the possibility that the answers to the questions posed above can allocate some degree of responsibility for the present inner violence in our society?

Putting things in perspective while addressing these questions and analyzing the degree of violence in our society, we must bear in mind that our country IS NOT, and has not been, as most countries suffering from internal violence are, disenfranchised by government upheavals; burdened by starvation levels of poverty; involved in territorial disputes with neighboring countries; or a country victim of ethnic atrocities.

On the contrary, our country is in fact a country that serves as a role model for most other countries for its tolerance, prosperity, political and economic stability. And still, our internal violence is an unresolved issue.

Our country has recently and repeatedly suffered self-induced violence in some of the most despicable of forms: massive school shootings by one of their own students using rapid-fire weapons against innocent schoolmates and teachers; disgruntled employees storming into their work place with loaded guns and perpetrating multiple killings to vent their anger. These horrific catastrophes have taken place unabated by any type of gun controls. Ours is a country where city violence and gang related shootings have become everyday events. It is a country where, in spite of the goodness of its people, endures all this violence and cannot pass laws to reduce it.

Each one of us must ponder these questions, find the answers in our hearts, follow our feelings and intuition…and do something about it. We the people can!

Here are a few quotes that may prove of value as you reflect on what was said in this chapter:

On trimming our ballast:

"People become attached to their burdens sometimes more than the burdens are attached to them" - George Bernard Shaw

"The yoke you wear determines the burden you bear" - Edwin Louis Cole

"The burden of self is lightened with a laugh at myself" - Rabindranath Tagore

On physical nourishment:

"The wise man should consider that health is the greatest of human blessings. Let food be your medicine" - Hippocrates

"The body is the soul's house. Shouldn't we therefore take care of our house so that it does not fall into ruin?" - Philo

"Preserving the health by too strict a regime is a wearisome malady" - Francois Duc de la Rochefoucauld

On intellectual and spiritual nourishment:

"I find television very educational. The moment somebody turns it on, I go to the library to read a book" - Groucho Marx

"Education has produced a vast population able to read, but unable to distinguish what is worth reading" - G.M. Trevelyan

"I cannot live without books: - Thomas Jefferson

"Reading is to the mind what exercise is to the body" - Sir Richard Steele

"We must use time as a tool, not as a couch" - John F. Kennedy

"Music is the divine way to tell beautiful, poetic things to the heart" - Pablo Casals

"Music can change the world because it can change people" - Bono

"I think music itself is healing. It is an explosive expression of humanity. It is something we are all touched by" - Billy Joel

On violence:

"Nonviolence means avoiding not only external physical violence but also internal violence of the spirit. You not only refuse to shoot a man but you refuse to hate him" - Martin Luther King

"I object to violence because when it appears to be good, the good is only temporary; the evil it does is permanent" - Mahatma Gandhi

"The main goal of the future is to stop violence. The world is addicted to it" - Bill Cosby

"Peace does not mean just putting an end to violence or to war, but to all other factors that threaten peace such as discrimination, inequality, and poverty" - Aung San Suu Kyi

"The philosophy of the school room in one generation will be the philosophy of government in the next" - Abraham Lincoln

CHAPTER IV

Angels 101 - Introduction to Angel Sightings

"Comedy is simply a funny way of being serious" - Peter Ustinov

Thus far we have concentrated on identifying the factors that have affected Angelic visitations, or at least, our ability to recognize such visitations. These factors range from our distraction from spiritual matters caused by the allure of the "in-control high" we derive from the use of many new technologies; to the information overload that we are all experiencing - this often being "empty information", like the "empty calories" we consume; to the instinctual and emotional numbness that we have developed as direct consequence of the first two factors; and to more practical issues such as the change of wardrobe that Angels have undergone in an effort to be up to date, but which we still fail to recognize, perhaps due to our false and archaic expectations of seeing them in traditional garments (tunics, wings, trumpets, etc...).

We have also reviewed some of the changes that we must undertake, individually and as a society, to be more attuned with our spiritual side, deemphasizing our material component. Namely, taking a holistic approach to life, including being more careful in what we eat, in what we think, and how we use our time. In short, we have to adopt the firm determination to shift our current priorities and our habits with the objective of recapturing and developing our spiritual nature.

We will return and explore these issues on a more specific manner as they fit into our narrative, but for the present time, I think the message has been sent out loud and clear, hopefully to a receptive audience.

Having now covered the basic background for Angelic absenteeism, I think it is time to transfer our attention to the Angels themselves, hoping to understand where they congregate / hang out, what they look like, and how we should go about looking for them.

Actually, embarking on an Angel sighting project is, in many ways, no different from embarking on a bold eagle sighting project. The same disciplinary prerequisites apply. But before exploring the similitudes, we both (author and reader), have to agree to the underlying premise that we are serious about wanting to encounter an Angel….or a bold eagle ☺; and are willing to make the commitment to persevere in our search.

A bit further down the road, you (the reader) will have to make a choice and decide which of the two, and Angel or a bold eagle, you want to sight. Although I will happily tell you in advance that there is a bonus in the proposed "sightings orientation program", for once you know the basics, you can apply them to both, and have matching, if not simultaneous results.

There are three basic practical elements that will facilitate our sighting efforts for both of these "winged" creatures. These are:

1. Knowledge of subject's physical description
2. Knowledge of subject's preferred habitat
3. Sightseer's proper training.

Let's start with the bold eagle (*Chaliaeetus Leucocephalus*), birds of prey:

<u>Physical description</u>: Large bird of the eagle family, classified as a sea eagle. At maturity (5-7 years) weights between 10-14 lbs. and has a wingspan of 72-90 inches, and a body length of 35-37". Females tend to be larger than males. Body covered with dark brown and black feathers; head, neck and tail have white feathers. Can reach speeds of 75-95 mph. when diving, and 40-50 mph. when gliding. Bold eagles can fly at an altitude of 10,000 ft. Their lifespan is about 30 years.

<u>Preferred habitat:</u> Native to North America. Build their nest on high trees near rivers or coast lines. Bold eagles are monogamous, and their territory spans from 1,500 to 10,000 acres, depending on prey availability. Their main diet is fish, but will consume other live prey.

<u>Proper training for the sightseer:</u> Developing a strong, healthy physic is highly recommended, as strenuous field walks in the wild are often necessary to locate a bold eagle's nesting ground. Adequate clothing and endurance to varying weather conditions are also critical. Patience and discretion are indispensable. Sightseer must often remain still and quiet in one position for long periods of time. Multiple field trips are usually required before achieving any success. Lucky encounters are a definite factor.

And now, let's do the same for Angels (*Angelus*), messengers of God):

<u>Physical description</u>: Members of the homo sapiens family, but originally suspected to be a mutant sub-species due to scientifically unconfirmed but well described sightings of Angels sporting large wings with magnificent white plumage - these appendages being an addition to their normal human extremities. Current sighing reports do not substantiate this avian characteristic. Albeit that alleged winged

peculiarity, Angels come in all colors (human race colors, that is), sizes, genders, and ages - just like human beings. Angels have no distinct features other than a peaceful countenance and a serene bearing.

<u>Preferred habitat:</u> Initially believed to be exclusively celestial dwellers, but prone to making sporadic earthly sojourns. Presently, perhaps due to their increased numbers (their population has risen proportionately to ours in order to maintain the same Angel-to-man ratio), they can be found in both, metropolitan and rural areas. Although Angels have fully integrated into society at all levels, they continue to show a strong proclivity towards staying close to fellow brothers in need, and will thus most likely be present around these.

<u>Proper training for the sightseer:</u> Patience and discretion are indispensable. Sightseer does not have to remain still and quiet in one position for long periods of time. Multiple field trips are usually required before achieving any success. Luck is a definite factor.

Other than these tenuous requirements, as baffling as it may sound, there is no formal training needed. It is all a matter of attitude, and openness to the possibility. It could be said that Angel sightings are pretty much a matter of receptiveness, good timing, and luck.

As to this last element, what I would say is that, although luck does indeed play a significant role, the more we open ourselves to the possibility of sighting an Angel; the more we see ourselves in our brothers; the more respectful and humble we are of other humans, the luckier we get.

"I feel that luck is preparation meeting opportunity" - Oprah Winfrey

"The most beautiful things in the world cannot be seen…or even touched — they must be felt with the heart" - Helen Keller

"You can get help from teachers, but you are going to have to learn a lot by yourself, sitting alone in a room" - Dr. Seuss

"There are people in the world so hungry, that God cannot appear to them except in the form of bread" - Mahatma Gandhi

CHAPTER V

My First Indisputable Visitation

"I am trying to shut up and let my Angels speak to me and tell me what I am supposed to do" - Patrick Swayze

After driving for more than one hour, it seemed that we were the only car on the road that morning. We had not seen more than 20 vehicles since we left Cahors after a fortifying breakfast consisting of freshly laid country eggs, a generously buttered crusty baguette, and two cups of strong black coffee. Not the ideal breakfast preceding a 3 hour drive in a narrow curvy road, but…..we simply could not resist the many gastronomic temptations that France, Perigord in this particular occasion, presents to the appreciative visitor.

Having the road to ourselves was a welcomed relief from the frequent inconvenience in rural roads of getting stuck behind a slow moving truck, or even a tractor in some of the more remote areas of the countryside. That morning, the road had been clear of all these hindrances, and we had been able enjoy the picturesque drive uninterruptedly at our leisure.

Our destination was Villeneuve-sur-Lot, where we were planning, after exploring on foot the town for an hour or so, to enjoy yet another memorable lunch. The morning was perfect. Clear blue skies, wild flower covered fields, and a warm breeze that could be felt rolling up from the Dordogne river bank on our left side.

I had been driving without a worry in my mind, simply enjoying the scenery, enhanced by Vivaldi's Four Seasons, which our youngest son, and faithful travel companion, had chosen for the morning drive and was playing in the car's stereo system. My only dilemma was whether to keep the car windows down and enjoy the fresh air, at the expense of the fidelity of the music, or to roll up them up and let the air conditioning system do its job. The other two passengers, my wife, and our son, seemed to be in the same contemplative mood, and there was hardly any conversation – each of us in our own space. The morning was, like the weather, perfect.

Thus relaxed, and perhaps even doing a bit of daydreaming, I was leisurely driving when suddenly, before entering a blind curve, without any forewarning, I was shaken up by the clearly agitated and loud voice of our oldest son - who had passed away in a car accident one year before, emphatically saying to me: *"cambiate de carril, viene un coche en sentido contrario!"*, which in English is: *"change lanes, there is a car coming the wrong way!"* (although our family is bilingual, at home we chose to speak Spanish). My instant reflex was to get off the road - which I did without giving any thought to the consequences, and steered the car into the wrong lane towards the other side of the road. Fortunately there was an open space between the road and the river bank, and I managed to stop the car there after skidding in some loose gravel. As I did this abrupt maneuver, a large truck, with the driver clearly distracted, crossed our path, going the wrong way in the lane that I had just abandoned.

There was no time for either my wife or son to utter a word as this was happening. I just heard both of them gasp as they saw me brusquely make what they thought was a crazy and irresponsible move, and then turn white as we all saw the truck drive over the road surface that we had just vacated. Everything happened so fast, that none of us spoke a word until after our car had come to a complete stop.

It took a few moments for all of us to catch our breath, and finally, my wife, still in shock and barely able to speak, asked: my God, how did you know…what made you do it? I simply responded that Javi had warned me. What??? They both yelled in unison….he told you…how?? "He screamed to me - I barely mumbled, I heard his loud voice just like if he was sitting right behind me. He told me there was a car coming the wrong way".

Lunch at Villeneuve-sur-Lot was not what we had planned. I am sure the food was delicious, but we were all too emotionally affected by what had happed to enjoy anything other than the wonderful peace we felt, and the gratitude that kept on swelling in our hearts with the knowledge that our special Angel had saved us from a horrific accident.

One year before, we had held his funeral ceremony in our parish church in La Jolla. The church was filled to its limits, with many people having to stand outside. Losing a young member of the community is always a painful remainder to all parents of the fragility of our lives, particularly the lives of our children.

The community proved itself to be supportive and generous beyond our comprehension. I say this, because it is important to acknowledge the solidarity and love that were shown to our family, even if I am still doing so 29 years after the event. Although I have to confess that most of the comforting words that were spoken to me on that day were lost in my head, clearly due to the state of shock in which we all were, some words, for some reason, did "register", affecting me profoundly, and I have, ever since hearing them, cherished them immensely.

That day on the road from Cahors, one particular statement came back to us as clear as the day when it had been spoken. One of the last persons to approach us after the service, was Tim Burns, the Headmaster of La Jolla Country Day High School, where our son had been a popular student. Tim had been very close to our son, and he and his wife, Kathy, had become a good friends of us. He said: "Today we are grieving because you have lost a son, but you should be consoled by the knowledge that you have gained an Angel".

Twelve months later, our Angel saved our lives.

"I believe in Angels, so it is simple" - Isabelle Adjani

"We shall find peace. We shall hear Angels. We shall see the sky sparkling with diamonds" - Anton Chekhov

"Life and death are one thread, the same line viewed from different sides" - Lao Tzu

"When I die, I shall soar with Angels, and when I die to the Angels, what I shall become, you cannot imagine" - Rumi

CHAPTER VI

Angels 201 - A Guide Path to Angels' Gateway

*"Faith is a knowledge within the heart beyond
the reach of proof"* - Khalil Gibran

Recognizing the presence of an Angel, or "Angel sighting" as I tongue-in-cheek described it in last chapter's title, requires one or more factors to be in place for what I call the Angel Equation Formula to be consequential in Angel apparitions.

Namely:

1. Need for comfort / assistance / protection / guidance
2. Belief and faith in Angels
3. Receptiveness to the Angel's message / action
4. Consent for the message / action to take root in ourselves
5. Acknowledgment of message / action with gratitude
6. Serendipity

It is essential to be clear on these factors, for in their absence, you will most likely reduce the opportunity of letting Angels into your life. However, by letting these six simple components take root in your intuition process, they can easily become the underlying pathway for bringing Angels into your life. They are all simple elements, but they do require full acceptance and consideration; it is important that you keep them in mind as you progress with your reading. And remember, they work synergistically, but independent of each other. It is not necessary for all six of these factors to be present simultaneously. The only ones that must always be present in the equation, jointly or individually, are Nos. 1 – *Need;* and/or 6 – *Serendipity.* At least one of these two MUST be present. As to the others, the more of them that are present in the equation, the bigger the likelihood of having an Angel visitation, but they are not an absolute requirement for the formula to work.

Expressed as Algebraic formulas, there are multiple variations. Here are some examples:

Sum of 1:6 = Angel
1 = Angel
1+2 = Angel
2+6 = Angel
1+2+3+4 = Angel
3 +6 =Angel
2+ 3+4+5+6 = Angel
4+6 = Angel

Or any expression of any factor, or combination of any of these factors, as long as #1 or #6 are present, including the most riddled equation of them all: 6 = Angel

Before delving into these factors one by one, which we will do in the ensuing chapters, It is important to first be clear on how we define Angels. The definition that we will be using in this book is as follows:

Angels are spiritual beings, mortal or otherwise, that fulfill - usually spontaneously and unannounced, a specific positive mission in our lives, when we truly need it.

What do I mean by spiritual beings….mortal or otherwise? I mean that Angel visitations can be in person, if the Angel is mortal; and if not, it can be in the form of a dream; a voice in our head; or a sign known only to us, unmistakably valid.

It is important to realize, accept, and embrace that in addition to the spiritual energy forms that may come to our aid from other dimensions, such as the great Masters; or as some of our close family members that have passed on; or as "free agents" that are "assigned" to us, such as Guardian Angels, there are vast numbers of living Angels existing in our present dimension. They are embodied in the form of "regular" people we encounter, but not always recognize or acknowledge.

Simply put, living Angels are advanced spiritual beings that we meet in our daily lives, and that, following their nature and their self-chosen mission, help us when we are in need of their particular gift. They are low-key, modest "workers".

They come in all shapes and forms, from all walks of life. To name a few, they can be nurses; teachers; social workers; philanthropists; or young children refreshing us with their innocence and goodness, giving us unconditional love, and often teaching us important lessons that sweeten our lives. Often, Angels are individuals that have been burdened with handicaps, maladies, or situations that we ourselves doubt we could overcome, but in their case, those burdens have metamorphosed into a special well-focused strength that empowers their lives and enrich ours with their example and generosity.

Our Angel may turn out to be our next door neighbor, who assumingly, is very much alive; or it can be, as I narrated in my story of the previous chapter, someone very dear to us who has passed on to the other side, and comes back in the form of a voice that confers protection to us at the precise moment that such protection is needed.

What is important to keep in mind is that such spiritual beings WILL present themselves to us in time of need. Have no doubt about this. Perhaps some of you can remember your early feelings as a child, and can identify with the little boy/girl that goes to school for the first time and is nervous and scared of being away from home, of being with people he/she never met before; all in a new and unknown environment. To that child, those can be stressful times; times of anguish, but often enough, he/she soon found a soothing and nurturing person, most likely a teacher, or the parent of another child volunteering at school as "den mom", that provided the necessary support. That person made the child feel safe, and helped the child adapt, even thrive in the new environment. That person was an Angel – not necessarily of a high rank, but a true Angel none the less. I think most of us had such an experience…but did we recognize that person as an Angel? Probably not.

A higher ranking Angel – or perhaps a better description would be, an Angel "of a more advanced spiritual unfoldment", may be the vocational nurse who diligently, and at the expense of a great personal sacrifice, volunteers, putting her own life at risk, to care for destitute children at a foster ward in a foreign country plagued by social unrest, or even in a civil war.

What about that friend of ours that spearheads a food collection drive every winter for poor families living in city projects with no means of getting a healthy meal, or even getting to the store in bad weather? Is she not an Angel to those families?

Like those people, I am sure you can identify many in your circle that are constantly putting their own personal interests aside, committing their time and actions to help other human beings. There are countless people quietly sitting in the background, ready to jump into action when they can be of help. They are what I call our Angels in disguise. They are very low profile, but very high action people that are part of a movement that can be described as "spreading the Angel fire" in our communities.

I have deliberately refrained from citing Angels from the "official Angelical canons", or giving examples involving the most visible and recognizable Angel figures of our times, such as Mother Theresa, Mahatma Gandhi or Oskar Schindler for the simple reason that few of us doubt their Angel qualities, even though even fewer of us, if any, have ever met such people. Thus, I prefer to talk about "ordinary" Angels. The type we may encounter ourselves. The type we could even become ourselves....there are Angel positions available, and God is taking applications every day. Maybe you should consider filling one out when you finish this book. Job acceptance is practically guaranteed. God is an equal opportunity employer. No age limits. No physical exam required. No language proficiency tests. No dress code. No fixed hours. Workplace of your choice. You are your own boss.

My objective is to show you that there are many Mother Theresas amongst us. They may be working their Angelhood at a smaller scale, but they are being Angels all the same. Rather than exalt the virtues of one particular Angel stemming out of millions of people we never met, I want us to focus on that one Angel manifesting out of the few hundred people that do cross our paths.

Very few of us have the opportunity of meeting a Theresa, or a Mahatma, or an Oskar, but we all have met John Doe Angel, and Jane Doe Angel. There are many Johns and Janes in our community, and it is our loss not to recognize them...and a greater loss not to emulate them, and help "spread the Angel fire".

Regardless of their status in life, these Angels are always unselfishly sharing part of themselves with us, expecting nothing in return, other than the resulting effects of the help they proffer and the goodness they impart.

If their example were to be followed by more of us, the world would be a better place. The potential is there. In fact, we all can, and should indeed, make an effort to help each other more. Essentially, we are all the same, we are all spiritual beings, whether we are consciously aware of, and sensitive and proactive to this fact or not.

It is fundamental that we keep this in mind constantly; that we live our lives with this realization as the core of our actions, and the compass of our conscious thoughts; that we recognize this in every person we meet; and that we cherish and respect everybody in these terms.

WE ARE ALL SPIRITUAL BEINGS. WE ARE ALL MANIFESTATIONS OF THE DIVINE. Color, gender, size, and socioeconomic status, are simply the outer props; casings for the soul in our present manifestation.

This is what Scriptures mean by "love thy neighbor as thou love thyself"; this is what we do when we say NAMASTE. We are recognizing the divine essence in the person we meet. We – our higher self, is acknowledging and greeting the higher self of that person.

NAMASTE. The moment we start living our lives under the full awareness of this truth, we open the gateway for Angels to pass and come our way.

"Thousands of candles can be lighted from a single candle, and the life of the candle will not be shortened. Happiness never decreases by being shared" - Buddha

"Try to be the rainbow in someone's cloud" - Maya Angelou

"Kites rise against the wind, not with it" - Sir Winston Churchill

"We know what we are, but know not what we may be" - William Shakespeare

CHAPTER VII

Angels 301 - The Angel Equation Formula

*"As my mind can conceive of more good, the barriers
and blocks dissolve. My life becomes full of little miracles
popping out of the blue"* – Louis L. Hay

Picking up where we had started in the last chapter, we know that we
need one or more of the following six factors to be present for an Angel
to come our way - or even better said, to realize that an Angel has come
our way:

1. Need for comfort / assistance / protection / guidance
2. Belief and faith in Angels
3. Receptiveness to the Angel's message / action
4. Consent for the message / action to take root in ourselves
5. Acknowledgment of message / action with gratitude
6. Serendipity

As a preamble to our review of each of these factors, I want to emphasize
that although most people may agree to all of them, they will probably
dispute their order, assigning factor No.2, *Belief and faith in Angels* the
first place; making it the cornerstone of all other factors.

However, I do not believe (this word again!) that to be the proper sequence because by making *Belief* THE single most important factor, we are in fact downplaying, or even obscuring the importance of a miracle by pre-accepting its possibility, and therefore preying/wishing/ waiting for it to happen – almost "knowing" that it will. And when it does…no big surprise!

Faith is a strong additive for miracle making. And this is fine - it obviously works; but it does not provide for the most dramatic scenario. Angelic visitations to believers do not seem to constitute, at least not to me, as powerful a miracle as having a non-believer experience such an event. *Believing* takes away some of the magic…some of the shock element…it takes away the turned-into-a-believer thunder element.

Whereas if we remove the *Belief Factor* as the main component of the equation - or even better, if we remove it completely from the equation, ceding the center stage to *Need*, the Angel visitation, if and when it happens, becomes an undeniable game-changer to the non-believer.

Having made this point, let's proceed to analyze each of the six factors of the Angel equation formula:

Factor No. 1: *Need for comfort / assistance / protection / guidance*

The definition of Angels that we are using in this book, *Spiritual beings, mortal or otherwise, that fulfill - usually spontaneously and unannounced, a specific positive mission in our lives, when we truly NEED it,* underscores the precedence of *Need* over the others factors of the equation in most circumstances.

I say in most circumstances, because Angels, having their own free will and their own particular missions, sometimes will manifest themselves to a chosen few for reasons not apparently related to *Needs* - or at least none that are readily understood by us. However, these spontaneous, *not-when-in-need* apparitions usually fall more into what I would describe as "prophetic" apparitions/revelations, and they are not particularly relevant to the more mundane discussion of "common" Angelic visitations that occupy our interest in this book.

Rather, let's go back to the most frequent and personable cases of Angel visits, those that take place as a response to the No. 1 factor, *Need*. This for example, can be a *need of comfort* or consolation when in despair; or when in pain caused by the loss of a dear one; or when depression takes root in our soul. This is when an Angel comes to our rescue. The Angel may come in our dreams, or he may come in the form of a friend that says the right words, like those spoken to us at our son's memorial service by the Head Master of the High School he was attending (see Chapter III).

Need of assistance is another significant "Angel magnet". I remember a friend telling me a story of being stranded on a remote rural road in Fiji with a flat tire, and neither tools nor jack during a tropical storm at night fall; not knowing where he was, or how he was going to fix the tire. His family - wife and young kids, were in the car and had all begun to panic, fearing the prospect of spending the night cooped up inside a rental car in the middle or nowhere; with no means of communication, and exposed to the many horrible scenarios that were beginning to play in their heads as the rain continued, and nightfall approached.

Then, inexplicably, from behind some trees, without any forewarning, a large, native person appeared with a large metal object in one hand, and what seemed like a rod on the other; a wide grin on his face revealing a set of shiny white teeth. What initially was a scary moment - my friend being startled and not knowing the intentions of this "apparition," quickly became a joyful event. The metal object in the stranger's hand turned out to be an old scissor-shape jack, and the metal rod, was indeed a metal rod...to help crank up the jack! He was there to offer help.

There was no common language, so my friend, in spite of repeated attempts to communicate via gestures and signs, never learned how or from where this person had materialized out of the bushes…and with a jack! Within fifteen minutes, this "apparition man", as my friend's kids had dubbed him, completed the entire maneuver of changing the tire, always smiling and uttering incomprehensible words accompanied by jovial laughter. As my friends drove off, they realized that there were no signs of any form of human settlements along the road for the next several miles, and there had certainly been none for a long stretch prior to their flat tire. Where had he come from…was the "apparition man" an Angel? I think he most certainly was…a mechanic Angel!

Need of protection and guidance are the other two main drawing cards for bringing Angels into our lives, as they perform these duties relentlessly from the moment we become their charge, hence the moniker Guardian Angel. We all have at least one and he/she takes care of us constantly. Sometimes we call them our "lucky star" or our "lucky charm", but regardless of the appellation, we have all felt their presence on more than one occasion.

These Angels are the ones that, for no apparent reason, stopped us from crossing the road when a car was going by too fast; prevented us from stepping on that loose stone that could have caused us to fall; dissuaded us from accepting that ride from a person that had a bad car accident right after we declined…they are the ones that made the hair on the back of our necks stand out just as we were going to step on that snake, or into that hole. They are the ones that made us see reason out of chaos in difficult times…showed us how to be calm in times of turmoil.

They are the ones that nurtured and consoled me when I was withering in a hospital and later in a convalescent home. They are the ones that gave me strength, fed me, cheered me, bathed me…kept me in touch with life, when life was ebbing and eternal sleep was beckoning. They sensed my *need,* and they materialized. They were my Guardian Angels.

Factor No.2: *Belief and faith in Angels*

As recently discussed, *Belief and Faith,* providing fertile ground, are great facilitators of miracles, but they are not indispensable for the manifestation of any type of miracle, and by extension, of Angelic visitations. In fact, ironically, it seems that is often to those of great faith that miracles are most elusive.

Perhaps this is so because the stronger the *belief* and *faith* of an individual, the lesser their *need* for miracles. Or perhaps, as true believers would contradict, they see miracles constantly, but do not make too much fuss about them. Miracles happen to them every day, and are part of their lives. As Albert Einstein said: *"There are two ways to live: you can live as if nothing is a miracle, or you can live as if everything is a miracle".*

Regardless, the presence of *Belief* and *Faith* becomes, if not already pre-existing, a major requirement after the fact, otherwise the miracle - the Angel apparition in our case, would not be recognized as such by the receiver; it would simply be written off as a coincidence, or as a lucky event. Furthermore, *Belief* and *Faith* become a synergic force with factors Nos. 3; 4; and 5 of the Angel equation, as we will soon appreciate.

Factor No. 3: *Receptiveness to the Angel's message / action*

This is a very simple and basic requirement, but one that is often the biggest deterrent for having an Angelic visitation. We are all familiar with the popular saying: *"You can lead a horse to the water…but you can't make him drink it."* How often have we seen a fellow friend, clearly in need of help to break away from an old habit, refuse time and time again to take that extended hand given him? He is not *receptive* to help, thus he cannot benefit from it.

Another old adage illustrates this point quite well: *"When the student is ready, the teacher shall come forth."* In other words, one has to be ready; one has to be open and *receptive* to possibilities. Possibilities will not become reality unless seriously taken as such. This is not the same as *believing,* or *having faith,* it is simply being open to receiving something outside of our ordinariness; it is a modest, but critical requirement. Once this requirement has been met, once *receptiveness* takes root, and is satisfied, *belief* and *faith* often follow.

Factor No.4: *Consent for the message / action to take root in ourselves*

In addition to being *receptive,* we must also give our *consent to the message, or action to take root in ourselves,* for if not, the entire Angel effort would be a complete waste of energy. To illustrate this point, let's go back to the example that we reviewed under Factor No. 3 (*Receptiveness*) regarding a friend that is in *need* of help to break away from a bad habit. But even if this friend is *receptive* to help, this help will do no good unless he gives *consent* for this help to take place in his life; unless he lets this help, this *message or action take root in himself.*

A further example: In order for a homeless person to find shelter (which he/she *needs*), that person must not only be *receptive* to finding shelter, but must also be *consenting* to accepting such shelter; *consenting* to be given protection.

Factor No. 5: *Acknowledgment of message / action with gratitude*

Although this factor is debatable as a requirement for "Angel sightings" (humor from Chapter IV - Angels 101), it is, in my opinion, indispensable for the overall business of Angel visitations to be relevant in our lives. It is deplorable, and in very poor taste - as it shows lack of humility, not to express gratitude to those that help us in life. It is our obligation to give proper recognition to all people and circumstances that contribute to our safekeeping and betterment. *Acknowledging and having gratitude towards Angels, is no different than it is towards anybody else.* It is not "demeaning" or "embarrassing" to tell a friend that you were helped by an Angel. Angels need recognition. Our support for them will increase their popularity. The more popular they become, the more frequent their visits will be. The more frequent their visits are, the better off we will all be. It is a win-win situation. Let's be ready to say thank you; to always express our gratitude.

Factor No. 6: *Serendipity*

This is what makes Angels so fantastically unpredictable. This is why pious conduct will not assure our entrance ticket to Angel stadium. This factor is the true wild-card in the equation. One never knows if and when an Angel will show up in our lives. *Serendipity* brings excitement to the equation, fueling, even trumping all other 5 factors, for we have absolutely no control over it.

Need, will most likely present itself in our lives at some point

Belief and Faith, come either naturally, or can be eventually acquired, especially in not-so-good times

Consent, can also be developed, particularly when faced with *Need*

Acknowledgement and Gratitude, will hopefully be present, and if not, they are attainable as part of our spiritual development

But, *Serendipity*…how can we "factor" it in the Angel equation? We can't. And not only do we have to accept its reality, we have to cherish it, for this is what makes the entire Angel equation so inscrutable to so many, and so simple to others.

"Life is really simple, but we insist on making it complicated" – Confucius

"I think miracles exist in part as gifts and in part as clues that there is something beyond the flat world we see" - Peggy Noonan

"The golden moments in the stream or life rush past us, and we see nothing but sand….the Angels come to visit us, and we only know them when we are gone" - George Eliot

"God not only plays dice, he also sometimes throws the dice where they cannot be seen" - Stephen Hawking

CHAPTER VIII

Matilda's Angel
A Short Story About an
Angel From The Other Side

*"There is always room for a story that can transport
people to another place"* - J.K. Rowling

Note: Names, and places have been altered in order to maintain the
privacy of those involved.

This Angel story is based on factor No. 1 of the Angel Equation
Formula: ***Need***, and factor No. 6: ***Serendipity***

The events that I am narrating took place many years ago, during the
1950's. Their story was revealed to me by impeccable family sources
that witnessed the occurrences. I make it a point in saying this, because
I do not want the time factor to render the experience as anecdotal, or
simply as part of a collection of family stories that are passed on and
retold time over time.

The location of the story is a small town in the state of Veracruz. It transpired at the home of a locally prominent family. Their house was a very large, old hacienda type property that had been purchased and remodeled by the family's patriarch, Don Juan, when he became prosperous, and was blessed with a growing family.

Matilda, the youngest child in the family, was born well over a decade after her brother, Jorge, who had held that positon until "Surprise Matilda" – as she had been dubbed due to her unexpected late arrival, made her appearance in the world. Jorge was preceded by four sisters, ranging in age from 14 to 20 years of age.

This significant age difference separating Matilda from her siblings placed her in the position being an almost single child, and resulted in her not having the same type of upbringing that the other, older children had experienced. Not only was she the youngest of the brood by far, but her parents were also not quite the same parents that they had been when they had their first child 20 years before Matilda's time. This span of years, and the rearing of four daughters and a son, had rendered Don Juan and his wife, Susana, a bit more "tolerant" and prone to pampering the youngest member of the family.

One cannot truly say that Matilda was spoiled, but she did have a lot more freedom to roam about the house and play wherever she chose, than her older, more restricted siblings had enjoyed. On the downside, she did not have brothers or sisters close to her age to play with, but not knowing any different, she was content to be by herself, and either explore the many rooms in the house - an activity she thoroughly enjoyed; or quietly spend time in the one room that was her favorite and had claimed as "her playroom", where she would spend hours every day absorbed by those games that single children learn to improvise.

It was on the ground floor, a bit apart from other rooms, facing the backyard, and adjacent to the formal living room, which was never used, and had the curtains always drawn shut to prevent the sun light from fading the upholstery. The room had served several purposes over the years - most recently as a forgotten storage room before Matilda's ownership claim, and was largely unused prior to its quasi-abandonment due to its awkward location, and the abundance of rooms in the house. It was full of hopeless, but to Matilda, wonderful treasures, ranging from pieces of old furniture; to long ago abandoned suitcases; to an old useless bicycle of unknown origin; to a collection of strange bottles; to unread books gathering dust…to various tools and accessories; a true menagerie of artifacts. It was perfect for Matilda's daydream adventures.

The house was built on a large plot of land, some of it properly kept in garden form; another portion as an orange grove; another as a chicken coop; and another as a vast, uncared for space where nature was allowed to take its course, which was in the form of exuberant tropical vegetation that not only intoxicated the eye, but provided a fertile habitat for many creatures - scorpions and venomous snakes not being the least common of them.

Now that the scenography has been provided, let us move on to the factual story:

On a given Sunday afternoon, after the habitual family supper, the "adult" members of the family, following long established patterns, went into the drawing room where coffee was served and conversation continued. Matilda, having being excused from this ritual, went to "her playroom", only to come back shortly, screaming that she had almost been bitten by a snake in her room. Don Juan grabbed a golf club and started to head for Matilda's play room, but Matilda stopped him saying that it was not necessary to take any weapon; that her "friend" had scared the snake away, forcing it to leave the room through the back door leading to the backyard.

Not knowing what to make of this, Don Juan followed his initial instinct, golf club in hand, ignored what Matilda was saying about the snake having been chased, and rushed to the "play room". He was not sure if he was going to find a snake, or if the whole thing was a product of Matilda's imagination; but he was not prepared to take any chances, knowing that poisonous snakes were quite common in the area, and once inside the house, one would never be sure to which room it had fled. This would not have been the first time that a snake had found its way into the main house.

Well, no snake was found in the room, but to everyone's bewilderment, the door leading to the backyard had clearly been opened, as evidenced by the unlocked double latch in the upper part of the door - which could certainly not be reached by Matilda, and which due to lack of use was rusty and difficult to operate. Only an adult could do such task.

The immediate reaction that all family members had was one of relief, but this was closely followed by one of displeasure and concern about Matilda's silly game of scaring people, resulting in a stern reprimand from the part of her parents.

Matilda however, insisted that there had been a snake, and that her "friend" had made it go away. Her story never fluctuated one bit from her first telling. Her "friend" had rushed the snake out of the room when he saw that it was going to bite her. The whole thing made no sense, but not wanting to pressure her any more than what the situation merited, neither Don Juan nor Susana, his wife, said anything else on that day. They were sure that a proper explanation about the open latch would be found on the following day after the initial bafflement was overcome by all.

Nevertheless, no explanation was found. Matilda continued to insist, naturally, but firmly, that her "friend" had made the snake escape through the back door. But what "friend"? There had been nobody in the house besides the family and the help, which had been duly questioned and cleared of all possible involvement. "My friend - Matilda insisted...the one that comes to play with me sometimes". After a few minutes of head-scratching, Matilda's parents succeeded in getting more information out of her regarding this "friend". It turned out that quite frequently Matilda would find herself in the company of a gentleman, a bit older than Don Juan, who would sit with her, watching her play, and keeping her company. When further questioned, Matilda offered to show them a picture of her "friend", the picture she had found in one of the suitcases in the room.

Don Juan had purchased the home from the family of a gentleman named Don Eustaquio, a wealthy land owner who had died in the home a few years earlier. Not having had any children, his wife had continued to live in the house by herself for a few months after Don Eustaquio's death, but eventually found the house overwhelming in size and memories, and decided to sell it and move to a smaller home. Don Juan had purchased the house and remodeled it substantially, but being a very large house, had kept some of the rooms untouched, and some of their contents were apparently still there after many years. The photograph of Matilda's "friend" proved to be that of Don Eustaquio.

"Stories have to be told or they die, and when they die, we can't remember who we are or why we are here" - Sue Monk Kidd

"The purpose of storytelling is not to tell you how to think, but to give you questions to think upon" - Brandon Sanderson

CHAPTER IX

Jonas' Angels
A Short Story About Two
Angels on This Side

"We are, each of us, Angels with only one wing, and we can only fly by embracing one another" - Luciano de Crescenzo

Note: As in the Matilda's story, names and places have been changed in order to maintain the privacy of the protagonists. The setting can be in any mid-size town on the west coast

The main characters are Jonas, the ailing, older friend; Pietro, one of his protector Angels; and Giulia, his other protector Angel.

All six factors of the Angel Equation Formula were present in this event: ***Need; Belief; Receptiveness; Consent; Gratitude;*** and ***Serendipity!***

"No, No! The adventure first...explanations take such dreadful time!" - Lewis Carroll

Jonas had "known" Pietro for some years, but had never really gotten to "know" him other than as a college friend of his son, who although a few years younger that Pietro, was much closer to him in age and lifestyle than Jonas was. It would be more accurate to say that at the outset of this story, Pietro and Jonas were close acquaintances...not really friends.

On the other hand, Jonas had known Giulia very well for many years. She was considered an extended part of the family, or even closer...she had been an Angel in Jonas' life on more than one occasion since they met more than 30 years back.

I will digress from the story briefly, but since this book is about Angels, I need to say that, from what I know about Giulia, another entire Angel book could (should) be written about her, and the many lives she has touched. Her timing is impeccable, always showing up - unsolicited, at the precise time and place, with the required assistance. Then, after doing her good deed, she quietly recedes into the background. That is her modus operandi – Angel behavior at its best! But as I said, she is subject of another book, and this story is only about the help Jonas received from these two Angels, so I will revert to our story.

Little did Jonas suspect the roles that these two people were about to play in his life, or of what laid in store for him as he boarded his flight to LAX from Guadalajara, for what he assumed was going to be a two week visit. Nobody could have predicted how these two people, one a mere acquaintance, would become his champions in his quest for health, and in his eventual repatriation to the U.S.

Jonas had been quite successful in business for many years, mainly as a residential developer in Southern California, and, being a healthy and active person, had always planned with his wife to retire as late in life as possible. However, in matters of real estate, as Jonas well knew, and in matters of health, as he dramatically found out, the adage that "timing is everything" proved to be a deciding factor in his life.

While still in his early 60's, thinking that he could continue working successfully for another 5 to 7 years prior to retiring, the "perfect storm" brewed, and struck Jonas's path in the 2008-09 foreclosure debacle. A combination of overinvesting in similar properties, and a few bad business decisions hastily made in the then existing non-forgiving-all-taking market, fairly well annihilated both, his intention to continue working, and his nest egg for eventual retirement.

After a few unsuccessful attempts to jump-start another business, which soon proved to be an impossible task in the face of the prevailing business climate - especially for someone of Jonas's age and business background, he began to search for alternative, "outside the box" ideas for his economic survival. It was during that search that another unforeseen element in the "perfect storm" materialized: He was diagnosed with cancer.

It was diagnosed as a "reasonably benign" form of cancer - if such an oxymoron can be conceived. However, the emotional and physical impact that this new revelation had on his life became a game changer for him. All priorities had to be reviewed and re-arranged; all business related actions had to be inevitably postponed. The main, and only focus became beating the monster, defeating the cancer - which he apparently did at the time.

The next step after "winning" the cancer battle was to find a suitable home that could be affordable to him and his wife, and where they could, contrary to all previous dreams, take an early and modest retirement, or, as he privately hoped, a hiatus from daily work. Guadalajara seemed to be a good alternative. It was safe; the cost of living was significantly less than in Southern California; the city was beautiful; there were good medical facilities; and there were daily flights to the U.S. This last factor represented a much needed psychological crutch to Jonas, as it provided him with incentive for dreaming of a comeback.

The decision turned out to be correct. Guadalajara proved to be everything and more than what they had expected. Their two primary concerns, health and cost of living seemed to be under control.

Unfortunately, a second "perfect storm" engulfed Jonas as he returned to California one year later for an intended brief visit to follow up on his medical condition. The cancer was back, and this time it came back in a much more aggressive form than originally thought. A new crisis quickly erupted. His health was frail; his savings had further eroded during the time spent in Guadalajara; his hope of starting a new business faded with each passing day. Jonas was desperate, he was facing the strong possibility of an "untimely" death. His wife was in a state of panic. The ensuing months were hell.

Eventually, the eye of the storm passed, and with the passing came the first ray of light…dim, flickering, but a light all the same. After a prolonged hospitalization, Jonas was informed that the prognosis was quite encouraging; he was beating the odds, but he had to remain under medical supervision in the area for several months to continue the treatments that were necessary.

The new challenge was to keep alive that flickering, dim ray of light long enough to find a solution that would allow it to grow, to shine. How to find the means to stay in California for the duration of the treatments… Medicare (thank God for it) would take care of the treatments, but what about the living expenses?

Both, Jonas and his wife *believed* in miracles, and they were both *receptive* to them…specially so when in *need* – as it is in human nature; but how would the much needed miracles of shelter and transportation materialize in California? Stones were turned; bank accounts were reviewed over and over in the hope of finding some overlooked balance; short term rentals were scrutinized hoping to find something decent that was affordable...meanwhile, the flickering light got dimmer and dimmer.

The one factor that was clear to them was that for economic reasons Jonas' wife should return to Guadalajara and move in with a close relative (another Angel), thereby reducing the cost of living in California to one person, Jonas. This decision was made in cold blood, at the expense of the emotional and love sacrifice that it implied. It had to be done, and it was done.

Suddenly, just as quickly as the skies had darkened, the sun came out... shining!
The *serendipity* factor in the Angel Equation came into play!

Pietro, upon learning of Jonas' predicament, contacted Fred, Jonas' son, and generously offered him a room for Jonas in his house. But why Pietro, one could ask; what relationship did he have with Jonas; and why was he offering Jonas his house? All these questions had a simple answer: Pietro was an Angel...and Jonas was in *need*. Furthermore, Jonas *believed* in miracles; was *receptive* to them; was *willing to accept* them as they came; and Jonas felt *gratitude*. All the factors of the Angel Equation Formula were present.

But more important to the backbone of this book: Pietro was simply following his nature, his Angel nature. Being an Angel is a big responsibility, and it has no escape clauses, so we have to understand that, following his nature, Pietro had no conscious alternative but do what was natural for him to do: offer Jonas shelter upon learning of his need.

Although Jonas suspected Pietro to be a "bit far out" for an Angel, truth being said, he did not have much of a choice. When the God dice were rolled for Jonas, they had Pietro's number. Thus, Pietro inevitably stepped up to the Angel plate, as it was his calling; and Jonas, following the same precept, gratefully accepted the offer - it was the miracle he had been praying for. They were each being faithful to their respective assigned roles in the Angel Equation.

What had made Jonas suspect that was Pietro was a "a bit far out" to be Angel? Well, for one thing, because his behavior and demeanor were not typically Angelic. Angels usually did not (or at least not according their portrayed image) curse, drink, carouse, frolic, burp, or tell people to f _ _ k off without any hesitation. Angel Pietro did all of those things – constantly…and got away with it. He was that type of person. He could do what others dared not, and cause people to laugh and love him for his irreverence. Living with Pietro turned out to be a lot of fun.

Who else but an Angel would take in his home the cancer-convalescent 67 year old father of a college friend? Nobody….except another Angel.

And that is precisely what almost happened! Giulia, when seeing that Jonas was growing more and more disillusioned with his situation, and was torn between foregoing the cancer treatments required, and head back to Guadalajara, or staying in California in a very low rent unit in a not very desirable part of town, called him and offered to share with him some space in the small house where she and another equally generous lady lived. This would have caused significant trouble and discomfort to both of them, but those words were never mentioned, and the offer stood on firm ground.

So then, after almost being "California homeless", Jonas unexpectedly had two generous housing offers to consider: One in Pietro's very comfortable home, providing Jonas a large soft bed in a nice, bright room with a view…and a TV…and a private bathroom to top it off – all for him…no sharing with anyone else; or a modest space in the den of the two lady Angels' love-filled home…causing severe discomfort to all. This was not a tough decision for Jonas to make.

Both offers were profoundly and equally appreciated. But Jonas, being a practical man, and not wanting to cause (as well as to endure) any avoidable discomfort, gratefully accepted - to Giulia's understandable relief, he was sure, Angel Pietro's offer, while also accepting Angel Giulia's offer to drive him to all his medical appointments and to his grocery shopping expeditions. This was a convenient solution, to say the least; and a well-rounded miracle, to say it better.

Regarding Pietro's positive, traditional Angel profile, and independent of the good deed he did for Jonas, it must be also said in Pietro's defense, that in spite of his rowdy habits, his Angel character was clearly manifested in his devotion and love for of his 9 year old son - another true Angel in the making, who lived with him at least half of the time, as per the joint-custody agreement Pietro had with his ex-wife. In fact, the agreement seemed to be quite liberal, for Pietro Jr. often spent weeks at the time at Pietro's home, giving an added dimension – a very nurturing one, to Jonas' boarding.

Pietro Jr. besides bringing the cheerfulness to the household that most children do, helped Jonas fill the void created by the absence of his own grandchildren, whom he hardly ever had the chance to see. Although he had grown to accept the fact that they were not close to him, he still missed them terribly.

In summary, Pedro and Giulia made the perfect Angel duo in Jonas' life. Their record will be hard to beat…that is, if anyone keeps score up above.

But the story does not end here, not by far. There are two more wonderful (miraculous?) things that blessed Jonas whilst living under Angel Pietro's roof. The first one involved gaining greater humility through gratitude, whilst having great fun. It meant learning to profit from the opportunity of being exposed to new ways of seeing the world through an unorthodox looking glass. Pietro, in addition to being a most generous, convivial, and discreet host, proved to conduct his household with down-to-earth practicality, and to possess a deep philosophical wisdom, which was always imparted - unpretentiously, in simple, one line sentences, in which almost half of the words were four letter expletives.

To his initial surprise, Jonas, being older; better read; "more sophisticated, and wiser" (?) than Pietro, soon found himself yearning for the daily evening chats they would have, during which Pietro never failed to fascinate Jonas with his unique take on life; on politics; on society; on sex; and on almost any other subject that came up, whether spontaneously, or surreptitiously instigated by Jonas, who in order to gain further insight on Pedro's always interesting opinions, and have a good laugh during the process, often did. Their conversations were not only revealing and instructive, but great fun as well.

Although disguised as a rogue, Pietro was true Angel, and a true teacher of basic, no-nonsense, practical thinking. What made him thus was that he was 100% genuine. No B.S. about him. He called things by their proper name. This was indeed refreshing. As days went by, and the shock value of the constant use of four letter words wore off, Jonas learned to appreciate Pedro more and more, discovering a well-educated and well-travelled gentleman, who for some reason of his own, had decided to wear the scoundrel mask to do his Angel deeds. If Zorro was entitled to wear a mask, why not Pietro? More credit to him for that. In fact, while making him more surreal, it made him more accessible and endearing...and Jonas respected him more for it. Gratitude grew on several fronts.

The second, very good thing that happened to Jonas during his tenancy at Pietro's involved prosperity. He regained strength and confidence for starting a new project. He applied himself rigorously to a new, different venture; the right doors opened; and he succeeded in getting a fresh start in life. He now, once again, lives happily with his wife - in great part thanks to the Angels that helped him when most needed. Such is their function, and Jonas' gratitude is eternal.

"What is coming will come, and we will just have to meet it when it does" - J.K. Rowling

"Hope is being able to see that there is light despite all the darkness" - Desmond Tutu

"We must accept finite disappointment, but never lose infinite hope" - Martin Luther King Jr.

CHAPTER X

Angels 401 - Mission Statement

"You have to work hard to get your thinking clean, to make it simple. But it's worth it in the end because once you get there, you can move mountains" - Steve Jobs

This chapter provides the final guide that will help you recognize the Angels amongst us as well as, and more important, enable you to soar amongst them. In contrast to the long prose that has been used throughout this book to make its mark, this chapter, following the main precept of Chapter III ("We Must Trim Our Ballast"), is presented in simple outline form – it is streamlined for maximum efficiency; to be used as a "personal instruction manual" for making the necessary adaptations in your life that will enable you to reach the objective at hand.

The outline is universal to all of us, But its individual points may not signify the same thing to everybody. It is up to each of us to "fill-in the blanks" and make our own personal evaluations and adjustments that are required to meet our goals.

It's presented in this manner because if you are at this stage of the book, you must have read all the previous chapters, and found resonance with their content. It means that you have made, or are in the process of making, some adjustments in your life, and that you are ready to fly under the power of your own wings - even if the initial flights cover short distances; or if unexpected turbulence is encountered; and even if some of the landings are less than perfect.

There is nothing more that can be didactically added to your quest. The final results are dependent entirely on you. The outline provided in this chapter, and the two Work Books that follow, will serve as your blueprint to "connect the dots" using the facts that we have reviewed in the previous chapters, and more specifically, following your heart's inclinations. The final discovery will be all yours, and the more you work on this quest, the more spectacular the results will be.

MISSION STATEMENT

To enable yourself to recognize and appreciate the Angels that come in contact with you; and in turn, to become yourself an Angel to other people.

STEPS TO ACCOMPLISH YOUR MISSION

1. REASSESS YOUR DAILY USE OF NON-WORK TIME

    a. TV; phone; social media; tabloids; gossip
    b. Quality family time; reading; meditating; exercise; hobbies
    c. Balance of technology vs. humanity

2. REASSESS QUALITY OF YOUR ACTIVITIES DONE IN NON-WORK TIME

 a. Watching cultural shows vs. fluff / reality shows (the "Krudatians / Honey Poo Poo" type)

 b. Watching real life socio-political news vs. gossip news (the "Red Carpet" type)

 c. Watching "happy" shows vs. violence filled shows (you know which)

 d. Listening to relaxing / inspirtional music vs. over-stimulating music (the Heavy Metal type)

 e. Reading worth-while literature vs. garbage / tabloids (you know which)

 f. Performing balanced social work vs. exclusively self-serving activities (Manicures; facials; Happy Hours…..etc…etc…)

3. REASSESS QUALITY OF YOUR DAILY NOURISHMENTS

 a. For the body, i.e. stay away from junk food; eat more organics

 b. For the mind and the spirit, i.e. be selective in what you read and watch; and be selective of your conversations and language used

4. OPEN YOUR HEART

 a. Follow your instincts

 b. Listen to your inner voice

 c. Trust yourself

 d. Be compassionate

 e. Do not overthink things

 f. Encourage the feeling of gratitude to take root in you

5. TRIM YOUR BALLAST (Physical and emotional)

    a. Maintain your "best" weight / eat healthy
    b. Discard any hateful feeling you may have
    c. Discard all bad memories
    d. Simplify your life
    e. Learn to forgive – put it in practice

6. ELIMINATE VIOLENCE

    a. In your home
    b. In your workplace
    c. In your leisure time
    d. In your thoughts
    e. In your language
    f. In what you view and read
    g. In your music
    h. Analyze and define your position on gun control

7. BE OPEN MINDED TO RECOGNIZE ANGELS

    a. In dreams and inner voices
    b. In friends and strangers
    c. In yourself – in your potential

8. REMEMBER THE ANGEL FORMULA

    a. Angels come when they are needed
    b. Believe and have faith in them
    c. Be receptive to their message / action
    d. Give consent for their message / action to take root
    e. Acknowledge with gratitude their message / actions
    f. Acknowledge and embrace serendipity

9. PRACTICE / PRACTICE / PRACTICE

10. KISS (Keep it Simple Silly)

"A child of five could understand this. Send someone to fetch a child of five" - Groucho Marx

"One day I will find the right words, and they will be simple" – Jack Kerouac

"Our life is frittered away by detail. Simplify, simplify" - Henry David Thoreau

CHAPTER XI

See An Angel – Work Book

"You have to take risks. We will only understand the miracle of life fully when we allow the unexpected to happen" – Paolo Coelho

This Work Book was created in an effort to facilitate your process of "Angel sighting". Although successful sightings cannot be guaranteed, the possibilities of such an event taking place are significantly enhanced by diligently following this Work Book.

Please note that reading, understanding, and willingness to put in practice the points outlined in Chapter X (Mission Statement) is a prerequisite for this Work Book.

There are three main tools that are needed for the successful completion of this Work Book. These are:

1. Your heart
2. Paper and pencil
3. The Angel Equation Formula

It is your responsibility to bring the first two items to the table. The third item, the Angel Equation Formula, should be very familiar to you by now, and you can use the following summary of the six factors to refresh your memory:

1. Need
2. Belief / Faith
3. Receptiveness
4. Consent
5. Acknowledgement / Gratitude
6. Serendipity

FOREWORD

Memory is a wonderful thing - it encompasses many aspects of our lives. Mainly, we have:

- Mental memory
- Emotional memory
- Physical memory

Once we have learned something, even if we forget it, learning it for the second time is usually easier than it was on the first time.

Example: You learn to ride a bicycle when you are 5 or 6 years old, you ride it with your friends in the neighborhood for a few years and then you stop. Thirty years go by without you ever riding a bike again, and then suddenly you have to ride one…and you can. Perhaps with a bit of hesitation, but in a few moments it feels like you have been riding all your life. Your body remembers it perfectly. Same thing with skiing, or any other activity that requires initial learning, once you master it the first time, the knowledge is always there. This applies to all three memory types that are mentioned above.

This is why memory can, if properly filtered, be our strongest ally for successfully completing this Work Book. However, memory, besides being a wonderful thing, is also a funny thing, for it often plays tricks on us and has us believe that events took place in a certain way, when they in fact did not; and other times refuses altogether to bring forth the information requested - but still, all events in our lives get recorded in our memory banks, and it is just a matter of finding the right "file" to be able to bring everything back.

Think of it as software that can be accessed pretty much the same way you access information with your computer by means of Google or similar search engine. You provide the key words to a topic, apply the right filters, and you can find a lot of information that you were perhaps not even aware of its existence.

When it comes to the emotional section of our memory files, things get a bit trickier, for we tend to ruminate over our emotional experiences, and rationalize our reaction to them before officially sending them to their corresponding file in our memory bank. We do this in order to justify to ourselves our feelings, and our conduct.

In this process of reviewing and editing our emotional experiences prior to filing them in our memory bank, a lot of stuff gets, if not deleted, encrypted; while other stuff, the pleasant stuff, gets neatly filed after it has been conveniently enhanced. This is how and where we put away our bad experiences – often hidden in a "locked" file cabinet. And this is also where we keep our enhanced and re-interpreted good experiences, but we usually place these in the upper shelf of the open files cabinet.

This where our heart comes into play: we are going to use it to access all of those emotional files and search for clues of possible past Angel sightings – although they were probably not recognized as such when they took place.

Once we find these clues, these feelings, we can nurture them back in our heart memory; we can "re-live" the event, and use the resulting emotion as a "detector" to search for a new similar experience, a new Angel sighting. Though it is possible that our emotional memory bank may not yield a believable, or even a suspect past Angel experience, the search process that we will undergo will open us to future sightings in ways that cannot be easily described, but which will be clearly felt.

To recap: We are going to use our heart as a filter, pretty much as we would use a filter if we were Googling for a used car, i.e. the filters for

Google would be: Make; Model; Year...etc...etc... The more filters we apply, the shorter the list of items that Google find, but the more specific they are to what we are searching. With the heart, the filters will be different, but the principle is still the same.

INSTRUCTIONS

This Work Book consists of five Exercises, each covering one or more of the six factors of the Angel Equation Formula. It is strongly suggested that initially they be done in the sequence in which they are presented, but subsequent work can be done in the sequence of your choice. We will be using our heart simultaneously as a search engine and as a filter, and if some of us feel an inclination to a specific factor in the Angel Equation Formula instead of the suggested sequence after having completed the Work Book at least once, then by all means, let's follow the heart, and go straight to that Exercise which beckons.

Please have your paper and pencil ready and make notations of each "memory / emotional entry".

Prior starting each Exercise take a 5-10 minute "let go" break during which you should stop all mental activity - release your daily worries. This ten minute gap is your personal quality time. Use it to disconnect from all around you. Focus on NOTHING...let there be a void... silence....only your breath and your soul. Allow all things to vanish... have no thoughts.

When you feel you are in that state of "nothingness", let your inner voice tell your heart that it (the heart) is in command for the duration of this Work Book. Surrender to it...do not allow your mind to dictate your feelings...do not pass any judgments...let your heart be your guide.

EXERCISE #1

Angel Equation Formula Factor(s):

- #1: NEED

(Remember to take the 5-10 minute "let go" break prior doing the Exercise)

PART ONE

TASK:

When doing this Exercise, spend some time and effort on each point, but do not try to force any memories - they may, or may not come back…and if they do, they will come back on their own, at their own good time. Do not force the issue. Please write down any memories and feelings that surface. Be as specific as you can, but do it naturally. You may want to do this as each memory / feeling recedes to give room to a new one, or you may prefer doing it at the end of the session. It is your choice, do whatever feels natural to you, but please do it and keep the record. And please understand that there is no wrong answer to any of the points. Whatever comes up from your memory bank is the correct answer…or, non-answer

1. Go back to your earliest memories as a child (5 to 12 years of age)
2. Try to resurrect any warm/happy feelings you may find
3. Focus on the strongest warm/happy feeling that comes up
4. Try to find out what brought this feeling
5. Do the same for any and all similar feelings that surface…one at the time

6. Now try to resurrect any feelings of fear or inadequacy…if it is not there, don't try to force it. Let it be…not everyone has the same feelings

7. Do you recall feeling NEED of anything….if so, can you define the NEED?

8. How did these feelings get resolved?

9. Do this for each one of these feelings

10. Is there a connection between the warm/happy feelings you first resurrected and these feelings of fear or inadequacy, or NEED?

11. How do you feel at this moment?

12. Did any faces or names come up during this process?

13. Focus on these faces and these names and see if you can bring them up over different stages of your life

14. Take a few deep breaths and try to develop a feeling of acceptance ad gratitude for all the feelings that surfaced and the people that accompanied them.

15. Let these feelings fill your heart

16. Give yourself a pat on the back and make sure you wrote down the relevant findings

EXERCISE #1

<u>Angel Equation Formula Factor(s):</u>

- #1: NEED

(Remember to take the 5-10 minute "let go" break prior doing the Exercise)

PART TWO

TASK:

Once you feel contentment and are at peace with this early period of your life, repeat the same process for later periods of your life. Depending on your current age, you may find it practical to break down this reflection process by decades...or you may prefer to break it down in segments according to benchmarks in your life, such as prior to college; during college; after college but before marriage; after marriage and up to some point, and then go on and on in this manner. It is really up to you. Do it in the way that is most natural to you.

Please notice that the outline points have been modified to incorporate NEED into them more specifically. This new form is the one to be used for all subsequent age stages, starting from your teenage years.

1. Go back to your earliest memories of the period chosen
2. Try to resurrect any warm/happy feelings you may find
3. Focus on the strongest warm/happy feeling that comes up
4. Try to find out what brought this feeling
5. Do the same for any and all similar feelings that surface...one at the time

6. Now try to resurrect any memories and feelings of NEED that you may have had in those years. Any form of significant NEED - the need to overcome fear; to regain good health; to solve financial issues; to solve social issues; to solve work issues….whatever relevant NEEDS you can bring to surface from your memory bank. The stronger the memory of having a NEED the better, but there is nothing wrong if NO memory of NEED manifests itself

7. How did this NEED get resolved?

8. Did someone help you resolve it, and if so, how was this done?

9. Do this for each one of the instances that you can remember being in NEED

10. Is there a connection between the warm feelings you first resurrected and the memories of NEED that have surfaced?

11. How do you feel at this moment?

12. Did any faces or names come up during this process?

13. Is there a relationship between these faces or names and the resolution of your NEED…is there a connection with the warm feeling you initially identified?

14. Focus on these faces and these names and see if you can bring them up over different stages of your life

15. Take a few deep breaths and try to develop a feeling of acceptance ad gratitude for all the feelings that surfaced and the people that accompanied them.

16. Let these feelings fill your heart

17. Give yourself a pan on the back and make sure you wrote down the relevant findings

At the completion of every Exercise, you should have notes on all the points covered. Do not try to interpret the memories and the feelings, simply acknowledge and embrace them. At the right time, it will all fall into place…your heart will let you know when that is.

Remember to do this for every age stage of your life that you have identified.

EXERCISE #2

Angel Equation Formula Factor(s):

- #2: BELIEF / FAITH
- #4: CONSENT
- #5: GRATITUDE

(Remember to take the 5-10 minute "let go" break prior doing the Exercise)

TASK:

Follow precisely the same methodology that you used for Exercise #1, with the variant that for this Exercise the same outline is used for all age stages. Please note that if the words BELIEF and FAITH are not agreeable to you in the context of this Exercise, feel free to substitute them with equivalent words that make you feel comfortable, such as "somehow knowing / having no doubt / having a feeling / being hopeful", or any other words that have resonance with you.

1. Go back to your earliest memories of the period chosen
2. Try to resurrect any warm/happy feelings you may find...they may be the same as in Exercise #1, but they may be stronger, or somehow "different"
3. Focus on the strongest warm/happy feeling that comes up, and see how it differs from the first time it surfaced...or are there new feelings this time?
4. Try to find out what brought this feeling
5. Do the same for any and all similar feelings that surface...one at the time
6. Now try to resurrect any memories and feelings of having had a strong BELIEF or FAITH in something in those years – even if

you felt let down afterwards; at this point it does not matter. All we are doing is trying to establish a connection with the feeling of BELIEF or FAITH. ANY BELIEF or FAITH on something or someone will do. Faith in your family; in your country; in your good luck; in yourself; in your mate…etc..etc.

7. Can any of these memories of BELIEF or FAITH be somehow related to the warm/happy feelings you experienced while engaged in the previous points?

8. Can you remember being in a difficult situation and somehow knowing that it was going to be resolved…..not quite knowing how, but still, BELIEVING that it would be resolved?

9. Did someone help you resolve it, and if so, how was this done?

10. Do you remember any unexpected favorable outcome that came unsolicited, but that somehow you had BELIEVED it would come about?

11. Do you remember ever feeling absolutely helpless about a situation, but still "knowing" that a solution would be found?

12. When reviewing the cases of NEED that you felt during Exercise #1, do you remember having BELIEVED that the NEED would be somehow satisfied…do you remember having had FAITH on a positive outcome…on an UNEXPECTED positive outcome?

13. Is there a connection between the warm/happy feelings you first resurrected in this Exercise #2 and the memories of BELIEVING or having FAITH that have surfaced?

14. How do you feel at this moment?

15. Did any faces or names come up during this process?

16. Is there a relationship between these faces or names and the BELIEF or FAITH feelings that surfaced…..is there a connection of these faces or names with the warm/happy feeling you initially identified in this Exercise?

17. Focus on these faces and these names and see if you can bring them up over different stages of your life

18. Take a few deep breaths and try to develop a feeling of CONSENT and GRATITUDE for all the feelings that surfaced during this Exercise and the people (faces or names) that accompanied them.
19. Let these feelings fill your heart
20. Give yourself a pat on the back and make sure you wrote down the relevant findings for each age stage reviewed.

EXERCISE #3

<u>Angel Equation Formula Factor(s):</u>

- #3 RECEPTIVENESS
- #4 CONSENT
- #5 GRATITUDE

(Remember to take the 5-10 minute "let go" break prior doing the Exercise)

TASK:

For this Exercise we are going to follow a slightly different method. You are going to use the notes you have taken for each age stage of each Exercise as your main guide.

1. Review every point of the outline for Exercises #1 and #2. Do not repeat the Exercises, simply go over all the points that you have already covered and let whatever new feeling or memory surfaces do so freely
2. Now please take out your notes and go over them, always using the outline points in each Exercise as a reference to each notation
3. Dwell for a moment on each feeling that this process evokes; whatever the feeling is, let it be
4. Ask yourself if you were RECEPTIVE to the feelings of NEED; BELIEF / FAITH at the time when they were originally felt
5. Ask yourself if you were RECEPTIVE to these feelings – now memories, when subsequently brought back in the corresponding Exercise
6. Ponder this for a moment. Take a few deep breaths and revisit your memory on these issues. How did your mind process the feelings….how did your heart process them?

7. Ask yourself how you feel about them now. Has your RECEPTIVENESS changed?

8. Has life made you more, or less RECEPTIVE to unexpected possibilities?

9. Are you RECEPTIVE to making adjustments aimed at augmenting your openness....your RECEPTIVENESS?

10. Take a few deep breaths and try to develop a feeling of CONSENT and GRATITUDE for all the feelings and memories that surfaced during this Exercise

11. Let these feelings fill your heart

12. Give yourself a pat on the back and make sure you wrote down the relevant findings for each age stage reviewed.

CHAPTER XII

Become an Angel—
Work Book

"Try to be the rainbow in someone's cloud" – Maya Angelou

This Work Book is THE most important single element of the entire book. Why is it so? Because it has nothing to do with receiving...IT IS ALL ABOUT GIVING.

Our desire and our RECEPTIVENESS to have an Angel help us when we are in NEED, is understandable; laudable; inspirational; critical for our spiritual life; and finally, if and when it happens, it can be a turning point in our lives, BUT... it is about US, about OUR NEEDS.

HERE WE GO BEYOND OUR NEEDS. Here we are not trying to find answers. We are not trying to get help. Here we are preparing ourselves to become such an answer, to become such a help for OTHER'S NEEDS.

This is what it is meant by "Soaring with the Angels" – becoming an Angel. Quite a challenge....and quite a reward!

FOREWORD

Although full understanding and ACKNOLEDGEMT of the MISSION STATEMENT specified in Chapter X, as well as full CONSENT to its requirements, and the resulting changes to our lifestyles that they will bring, are prerequisites for a successful completion of this Work Book, the fundamental ingredient...the one that you will bring to the table, is your genuine and unwavering desire to make a positive difference in other people's life.

Some of you might say that such a requirement is so obvious, that it should be considered a done deal. However, having a desire to be good, and being good is not the same. Desiring to do a good deed is not enough to make a significant difference in someone's life. We must go beyond having a desire, we must act upon it. It requires sacrificing a portion of our time; also some of our resources. It requires recognizing a NEED in other people's lives, especially when such a condition is veiled to the casual observer – as it often is, and then providing the means to resolve such NEED in a way that the dignity of the beneficiary is not diminished or affected in any manner.

Some people are natural Angels, but this is not the case for most of us. We have to work hard at it. On the positive side, once we manage to have a breakthrough helping someone, we become better at it, and we can do more good with more ease. The first time is often the hardest. Sometimes we simply do not know what to do, or where to start.

Well, the answer is simple: Let's start with this Work Book.

INSTRUCTIONS

As in the previous Work Book (Angel Sightings), you will need some tools. These are:

- Your heart
- Paper and pencil

We will be using a very similar outline to the one used in for the MISSION STATEMENT in Chapter X but the sequence of the Exercises is not the same. The objective is to (a) prepare ourselves to be in the right Angel frame of mind; and (b), to illustrate ways in which we can achieve such role.

As we move from one section of this outline to the next, you must be sure to understand fully what each step entails. It is advisable to write notes as you make your way through the outline. It may be helpful if these notes are written in a "private diary" type of format, i.e. notes to yourself… reflections on your feelings…on your insights…on your intentions.

You will find that going back to Chapters II ("We Must Put Our Hearts to Full Use"), and III ("To Fly We Must Trim Our Ballast"), and reviewing their contents as you make your way through this Work Book will prove very beneficial. It will help you "open up" as you obtain a deeper understanding of the task at hand. The concepts presented in those chapters have most likely already made an impact on you, and re-reading them will augment their resonance in your heart.

Taking periodic 5-10 minute "let go" breaks is very beneficial whilst completing the exercises in this Work Book.

"We must go beyond the constant clamor of ego, beyond the tools of logic and reason, to the still, calm place within us: the realm of the soul" - Depak Chopra

EXERCISE #1

OPEN YOUR HEART

This first Exercise is truly the key to the whole puzzle of how to help other people. We have all the answers, and compassion is already embedded in our heart, but we have to nurture them and allow them to flourish. Review each of the points below, allowing yourself the time and space to reach deep inside and assimilate their respective message and take a position.

    a.   Follow your instincts
    b.   Listen to your inner voice
    c.   Trust yourself - all the answers are already in your heart, in your higher self
    d.   Be compassionate
    e.   Do not overthink things – remember the KISS principle
    f.   Encourage gratitude to take root in you - It will give you a nice warm/happy feeling

All of these are easy, simple points, but do not let their simplicity trick you into taking the easy way out. You REALLY have to dwell on each one, let your feelings swell to the point that you know for certain that you have reached the point of no return – the point where you have clarity on each of the issues at hand. Write down in your "diary" all the feelings and emotions that surfaced…Did you feel any change within you taking place? The results obtained are in direct proportion to the effort given.

These considerations apply to all the Exercises in this WORK BOOK

EXERCISE #2

TRIM YOUR BALLAST

(Remember to take your 5-10 minute "let go" break)

Achieving this action proffers what can be described as an elliptical benefit; a prize within a prize. To best help others, we have to be emotionally and mentally free of personal encumbrances; concurrently, this condition is more readily achieved as we endeavor to help others. Thus, by extension, the more good we do for others, the more good we do for ourselves, which in turn results in an increase to our capacity to do more good to others.

"Feel" each one of the four points in this section, and let your heart make the resolutions. We have gone over all of these points before (see Chapter III).

a. Discard any hateful feeling you may have – this is the time and place to do it!
b. Discard all bad memories – not as difficult as it first seemed
c. Simplify your life – this practice alone will make you a much happier person
d. Learn to forgive – put it in practice

Remember: The results obtained are in direct proportion to the effort given.

EXERCISE #3

REASSESS YOUR DAILY USE AND QUALITY OF NON-WORK TIME
(5-10 minute "let go" break?)

Make a commitment to your objective of becoming an Angel to those in NEED. To do this, you must re-prioritize your use of time, your focus of interest. You must make a shift from the position of YOU being the biggest priority - with no close second place, to seeing yourself in others, and loving them as such. To make this work, you have to review and amend (when necessary) your use of time.

    a.   Increase your quality family time. Home is the first place where you should do good.

    b.   Make time for doing "third party" good deeds. Examples: enroll as a volunteer in a convalescent home; or join "meals on wheels". The purpose of this is not only to help others, but to put you in the right path; to "open your heart" to the wonders of helping others.

    c.   Read only worth-while literature. Use this simple test to determine if the material you are reading meets the desired criteria:

        (1) Will it make you a better person?

        (2) Will it further your education?

        (3) Will it inform you of significant news?

        (4) Will it give you a healthy break from your daily chores?

If the answer is yes to any of these questions, or similar ones, then by all means read the material, and try to incorporate more of (1) and (2).

    d.   Develop the habit of seeing the goodness in everyone you meet, while avoiding passing any judgment on anybody. NAMASTE

EXERCISE # 4

PRACTICE, PRACTICE, and PRACTICE

- This Work Book IS NOT a do-it-once-and-it's-over type of Work Book
- This is a Work Book that must be done EVERY DAY, for many days
- You cannot reasonable expect to reach the moon on your first attempt...you have to PRACTICE
- You have to shed layer by layer of past bad experiences
- You have to gain layer by layer the goodness that you will eventually impart onto others
- It is a life changing event....and NEVER forget that it is all up to YOU.

MAKE YOUR COMMITMENT TODAY - THE FINISH LINE WILL BE CLOSER THAN IF YOU START TOMORROW

"If you are in the luckiest one percent of humanity, you owe it to the rest of humanity to think about the other 99 percent"- Warren Buffet

"Every man is guilty of all the good he did not do" – Voltaire

"With charity you give love, so don't give just money, but reach out with your hands instead" – Mother Theresa

"We only have what we give" - Isabel Allende

"If you go out and make good things happen, you will fill the world with hope…you will fill yourself with hope" – Barak Obama

If you would like to establish contact with other Angels, or if you have any questions, stories or suggestions that you would like to share, please visit www.myangelprojects.com or email info@myangelprojects.com

LIST OF QUOTES USED
THROUGHOUT THE BOOK

PREFACE

"Humor is something that thrives between man's aspirations and his limitations. There is more logic in humor than in anything else because, you see, humor is truth" - Victor Borge

"At the center of your being you have the answer; you know who you are, and you know what you want" - Lao Tzu

"Be faithful to that which exists within yourself" - Andre Gide

"Imagination was given to man to compensate him for what he is not, and a sense of humor to console him for what he is" - Francis Bacon

CHAPTER I

The Reason Angels Went the Way of Blockbuster

"It has become apparently obvious that our technology has exceeded our humanity" - Albert Einstein

"We are born, we live for a brief instant, and we die. It's been happening for a long time. Technology is not changing it much – if at all" - Steve Jobs

"Technological society has succeeded in multiplying the opportunities for pleasure, but it has great difficulty generating joy" - Pope Paul IV

"We have more media than ever and more technology in our lives. It's supposed to help us communicate, but it has the opposite effect of isolating us" - Tracy Chapman

"I think technology really increased human ability. But technology cannot produce compassion" - Dalai Lama

"If we continue to develop our technology without wisdom or prudence, our servant may prove to be our executioner" - Omar N. Bradley

"The internet is so big, so powerful, that for some people it is a complete substitute for life" - Andrew Brown

"I force people to have coffee with me, just because I don't trust that a friendship can be maintained without any other senses besides a computer or cell phone screen" - John Cusack

"You affect the world by what you watch" - Tim Berners-Lee

CHAPTER II

We Must Put Our Hearts to Full Use

"And now, here is my secret, a very simple secret: it is only with the heart that one can see rightly, what is essential is invisible to the eye" - Antoine de Saint-Exupery

"There are receptors to these molecules in your Immune system, in your gut and in your heart. So when you say 'I have a gut feeling' or 'my heart is

sad' or 'I am bursting with joy' you are not speaking metaphorically. You are speaking literally" - Depak Chopra

"Absence of evidence is not evidence of absence" - Carl Sagan

"I never get the accountants in before I start up a business. It's done on gut feeling, especially if I see that they are taking the mickey out of the consumer" - Sir Richard Branson

"Your time is limited….have the courage to follow your heart and intuition"- Steve Jobs

"There is no instinct like that of the heart" – Lord Byron

"Everyone has been made for some particular work, and the desire for that work has been put in every heart" - Rumi

"Only do what your heart tells you" – Princes Diana

"Wherever you go, go with all your heart" - Confucius

CHAPTER III

To Fly, We Must First Trim Our Ballast

"Believe you can, and you are halfway there" - Theodore Roosevelt

"The yoke you wear determines the burden you bear" - Edwin Louis Cole

"People become attached to their burdens sometimes more than the burdens are attached to them" - George Bernard Shaw

"The burden of self is lightened with a laugh at myself" - Rabindranath Tagore

On Physical Nourishment:

"The wise man should consider that health is the greatest of human blessings. Let food be your medicine" - Hippocrates

"The body is the soul's house. Shouldn't we therefore take care of our house so that it does not fall into ruin?" - Philo

"Preserving the health by too strict a regime is a wearisome malady" - Francois Duc de la Rochefoucauld

On Intellectual and Spiritual Nourishment:

"Education has produced a vast population able to read, but unable to distinguish what is worth reading" - G.M. Trevelyan

"I cannot live without books: - Thomas Jefferson

"Reading is to the mind what exercise is to the body" - Sir Richard Steele

"I find television very educational. The moment somebody turns it on, I go to the library to read a book" - Groucho Marx

"We must use time as a tool, not as a couch" - John F. Kennedy

"Music is the divine way to tell beautiful, poetic things to the heart" - Pablo Casals

"Music can change the world because it can change people" - Bono

"I think music itself is healing. It is an explosive expression of humanity. It is something we are all touched by" - Billy Joel

On Violence:

"I object to violence because when it appears to be good, the good is only temporary; the evil it does is permanent" - Mahatma Gandhi

"Nonviolence means avoiding not only external physical violence but also internal violence of the spirit. You not only refuse to shoot a man but you refuse to hate him" - Martin Luther King

"The main goal of the future is to stop violence. The world is addicted to it" - Bill Cosby

"Peace does not mean just putting an end to violence or to war, but to all other factors that threaten peace such as discrimination inequality and poverty" - Aung San Suu Kyi

"The philosophy of the school room in one generation will be the philosophy of government in the next" - Abraham Lincoln

CHAPTER IV

Angels 101 - Introduction to Angel Sightings

"Comedy is simply a funny way of being serious" - Peter Ustinov

"I feel that luck is preparation meeting opportunity" - Oprah Winfrey

"The most beautiful things in the world cannot be seen...or even touched — they must be felt with the heart" - Helen Keller

"Your can get help from teachers, but you are going to have to learn a lot by yourself, sitting alone in a room" - Dr. Seuss

"There are people in the world so hungry, that God cannot appear to them except in the form of bread" - Mahatma Gandhi

CHAPTER V

My First Indisputable Visitation

"I am trying to shut up and let my Angels speak to me and tell me what I am supposed to do" - Patrick Swayze

"I believe in Angels, so it is simple" - Isabelle Adjani

"We shall find peace. We shall hear Angels. We shall see the sky sparkling with diamonds" - Anton Chekhov

"Life and death are one thread, the same line viewed from different sides" - Lao Tzu

"When I die, I shall soar with Angels, and when I die to the Angels, what I shall become, you cannot imagine" - Rumi

CHAPTER VI

Angels 201 - A Guide Path to Angels' Gateway

"Faith is a knowledge within the heart beyond the reach of proof" - Khalil Gibran

"Thousands of candles can be lighted from a single candle, and the life of the candle will not be shortened. Happiness never decreases by being shared" -Buddha

"Try to be the rainbow in someone's cloud" - Maya Angelou

"Kites rise against the wind, not with it" - Sir Winston Churchill

"We know what we are, but know not what we may be" - William Shakespeare

CHAPTER VII

Angels 301 - The Angel Equation Formula

"As my mind can conceive of more good, the barriers and blocks dissolve. My life becomes full of little miracles popping out of the blue" - Louis L. Hay

"There are two ways to live: you can live as if nothing is a miracle, or you can live as if everything is a miracle" - Albert Einstein

"Life is really simple, but we insist on making it complicated" - Confucius

"I think miracles exist in part as gifts and in part as clues that there is something beyond the flat world we see" - Peggy Noonan

"The golden moments in the stream or life rush past us, and we see nothing but sand....the Angels come to visit us, and we only know them when we are gone" - George Eliot

"God not only plays dice, he also sometimes throws the dice where they cannot be seen" - Stephen Hawking

CHAPTER VIII

Matilda's Angel

"There is always room for a story that can transport people to another place" - J.K. Rowling

"Stories have to be told or they die, and when they die, we can't remember who we are or why we are here" - Sue Monk Kidd

"The purpose of storytelling is not to tell you how to think, but to give you questions to think upon" - Brandon Sanderson

CHAPTER IX

Jonas' Angel

"We are, each of us, Angels with only one wing, and we can only fly by embracing one another" - Luciano de Crescenzo

"No, No! The adventure first...explanations take such dreadful time!" - Lewis Carroll

"What is coming will come, and we will just have to meet it when it does" - J.K. Rowling

"Hope is being able to see that there is light despite all the darkness" - Desmond Tutu

"We must accept finite disappointment, but never lose infinite hope" - Martin Luther King Jr.

CHAPTER X

Angels 401 - Mission Statement

"You have to work hard to get your thinking clean, to make it simple. But it's worth it in the end because once you get there, you can move mountains" - Steve Jobs

"A child of five could understand this. Send someone to fetch a child of five" - Groucho Marx

"One day I will find the right words, and they will be simple"..-..Jack Kerouac

"Our life is frittered away by detail. Simplify, simplify" - Henry David Thoreau

CHAPTER XI

See an Angel WORK BOOK

"You have to take risks. We will only understand the miracle of life fully when we allow the unexpected to happen"..-.Paolo Coelho

"The marvels of daily life are exciting; no movie director can arrange the unexpected that you find in the street" - Robert Doisneau

"If you do not expect the unexpected, you will not find it, for it is not to be reached by search or trail" - Heraclitus

"God can cause opportunity to find you. He has unexpected blessings where you suddenly meet the right person, or suddenly your health improves, or

suddenly you are able to pay off your house. That is God shifting things in your favor" - Joel Osteen

CHAPTER XII

Become an Angel WORK BOOK

"Try to be the rainbow in someone's cloud" - Maya Angelou

"We must go beyond the constant clamor of ego, beyond the tools of logic and reason, to the still, calm place within us: the realm of the soul" - Depak Chopra

"If you are in the luckiest one percent of humanity, you owe it to the rest of humanity to think about the other 99 percent" - Warren Buffet

"Every man is guilty of all the good he did not do" - Voltaire

"With charity you give love, so don't give just money, but reach out with your hands instead" - Mother Theresa

"We only have what we give" - Isabel Allende

"If you go out and make good things happen, you will fill the world with hope…you will fill yourself with hope" - Barak Obama

MY ANGEL ROSTER

AleL*Alex*AlfonsoF*Amber*Anni*AnthonyH*BillF*Blanca*Bochis*
Bonnie*CharlieL*Cynthia*DianaA*Djamal*ElenaK*Ferro*Finn*
GastonL*Gely*Gero*Ginger*Gloria*Hugh*Isa*Javi*JefeJuancho*Julia*
KarenH*Kelley*KathyT*KikeL*KrishnaR*Lacho*LaloL*MaggieA*
MariaElena*Nicole*PeterP*Raphael*Rosamelia*SilviaB*SusaB*Susan*
Toto*Yola*AleL*Alex*AlfonsoF*Amber*Anni*AnthonyH*BillF*Blanca*
Bochis*Bonnie*CharlieL*Cynthia*DianaA*Djamal*ElenaK*Ferro*
Finn*GastonL*Gely*Gero*Ginger*Gloria*Hugh*Isa*Javi*JefeJuancho*
Julia*KarenH*Kelley*KathyT*KikeL*KrishnaR*Lacho*LaloL*
MaggieA*MariaElena*Nicole*PeterP*Raphael*Rosamelia*SilviaB*
SusaB*Susan*Toto*Yola*AleL*Alex*AlfonsoF*Amber*Anni*AnthonyH*
BillF*Blanca*Bochis*Bonnie*CharlieL*Cynthia*DianaA*Djamal*
ElenaK*Ferro*Finn*GastonL*Gely*Gero*Ginger*Gloria*Hugh*Isa*
Javi*JefeJuancho*Julia*KarenH*Kelley*KathyT*KikeL*KrishnaR*
Lacho*LaloL*MaggieA*MariaElena*Nicole*PeterP*Raphael*
Rosamelia*SilviaB*SusaB*Susan*Toto*Yola*AleL*Alex*AlfonsoF*
Amber*Anni*AnthonyH*BillF*Blanca*Bochis*Bonnie*CharlieL*
Cynthia*DianaA*Djamal*ElenaK*Ferro*Finn*GastonL*Gely*Gero*
Ginger*Gloria*Hugh*Isa*Javi*JefeJuancho*Julia*KarenH*Kelley*
KathyT*KikeL*KrishnaR*Lacho*LaloL*MaggieA*MariaElena*Nicole*
PeterP*Raphael*Rosamelia*SilviaB*SusaB*Susan*Toto*Yola*AleL*Alex*
AlfonsoF*Amber*Anni*AnthonyH*BillF*Blanca*Bochis*Bonnie*
CharlieL*Cynthia*DianaA*Djamal*ElenaK*Ferro*Finn*GastonL*
Gely*Gero*Ginger*Gloria*Hugh*Isa*Javi*JefeJuancho*Julia*KarenH*
Kelley*KathyT*KikeL*KrishnaR*Lacho*LaloL*MaggieA*MariaElena*
Nicole*PeterP*Raphael*Rosamelia*SilviaB*SusaB*Susan*Toto*Yola*
AleL*Alex*AlfonsoF*Amber*Anni*AnthonyH*BillF*Blanca*Bochis*
Bonnie*CharlieL*Cynthia*DianaA*Djamal*ElenaK*Ferro*Finn*
GastonL*Gely*Gero*Ginger*Gloria*Hugh*Isa*Javi*JefeJuancho*Julia*
KarenH*Kelley*KathyT*KikeL*KrishnaR*Lacho*LaloL*MaggieA*
MariaElena*Nicole*PeterP*Raphael*Rosamelia*SilviaB*SusaB*Susan*
Toto*Yola*AleL*Alex*AlfonsoF*Amber*Anni*AnthonyH*BillF*Blanca*
Bochis*Bonnie*CharlieL*Cynthia*DianaA*Djamal*ElenaK*Ferro*
Finn*GastonL*Gely*Gero*Ginger*Gloria*Hugh*Isa*Javi*JefeJuancho*
Julia*KarenH*Kelley*KathyT*KikeL*KrishnaR*Lacho*LaloL*
MaggieA*MariaElena*Nicole*PeterP*Raphael*Rosamelia*SilviaB*SusaB*
Susan*Toto*Yola*AleL*Alex*AlfonsoF*Amber*Anni*AnthonyH*BillF*

ABOUT THE AUTHOR, AND ABOUT THIS BOOK

"Believe that life is worth living, and your belief
will help create the fact" - Wiliam James

It all began with a call to 911 on a late Sunday night during the summer of 2013. The arrival of the paramedics and the ubiquitous fire truck, announced by their loud sirens, are always a portent of bad news to any neighborhood. But in this case, to the author, it was a much welcomed relief - it was the end to his position of denial.

After stubbornly enduring (foolishly, he later admitted) several days of pain and increasing difficulty in eliminating liquids, as well as suffering from other disconcerting complications believed to be the result of an allergic reaction to medication, the moment of facing reality had arrived for him. He was not immortal…he could no longer bear the pain. He badly needed….and finally accepted, medical attention.

No more pretending that everything was fine. The truth and its consequences had to be faced. He could not stand the pain any longer, and the realization that there was something seriously wrong hit him like a brick on the head as he was being transported in the ambulance. Once admitted into the emergency room at Scripps Memorial Hospital in La Jolla, CA, he completely surrendered, and allowed the "system" to take over….and what a wonderful "system" it turned out to be.

What he assumed was going to be a relatively short stay in the emergency room, evolved into admittance to the Hospital that night in preparation for a surgical procedure the following early morning, and then a month long internment in the hospital – an advanced cancer that had metastasized throughout the skeletal frame was discovered. Other serious complications developed.

Although the medical care given him was the absolute best that any patient could hope for, his situation was so advanced that the prognosis was very dire; the doctors were not sure for how long he was going to live.

At the end of the second week, after a multitude of tests and consultations amongst the many doctors involved, his wife of 45 years, and his eldest son were confronted with the facts of his precarious condition – they were advised to consider hospice care. There did not seem to be much more that could be done for him at the hospital. The end of his life in a matter of weeks seemed eminent.

However, contrary to the medical prognosis, he never doubted a positive outcome. He possessed the complete and unwavering certainty that he was going to be fine. He knew….rather, he felt, there was a higher power taking over his life, and he was certain that he was healing; that he should not give up.

While bedridden for weeks in the hospital, not quite unconscious, but certainly not fully conscious, he sensed a warm and loving "presence" engulfing him. It was both, nurturing and soothing. It was a presence of love and tranquility. It was first felt during a visit by a friend, a senior member of the Hospital's administration staff, who asked him if she could stand by his bedside and pray for him whilst she "passed energy" on to him by running her hands a few inches above his body. Something happened during those few minutes of "passing energy" and praying. He felt a "presence"….a deep love…a profound sense of peace…he "knew" he was going to be fine.

This feeling never left him from that moment. It gave him peace and strength, making him receptive to the loving energy that was constantly present in the room. It was continuously reinforced with the care given to him by so many wonderful people at the hospital, and later at the rehabilitation center where he was sent after four weeks to regain enough strength to walk, and to eventually be able to wash and dress by himself without assistance….and go home!

Maybe it was then that the decision to write this book was made, maybe the decision came later, and only the seeds were planted then….it does not really matter. The fact is that one year after having been almost "written off", the author, still alive and well, felt compelled to write this book - not to tell his medical story; not as a quest for catharsis; but to give testimony of what he learned (and "unlearned") during his illness. Not the least of which was a clear, and much needed personal reminder of the existence of Angels, for he had previously encountered several throughout his life – some in the flesh, others in spirit, but had gradually "filed and let go" of them in his memory bank as years went by and their relevance dwindled in proportion to the increase of the complacency that accompanies what we refer to as "the good life".

Thus, this book is the author's small way of expressing his gratitude to the Angels that protected, guided, and made him refocus on priorities, hoping that in the process, he can help some readers recognize and appreciate their personal Angels, allowing them to do their job, while we do ours.